For John
(Gift from God)
whose footsteps graced this earth
1963–2001.

What is love?
The infinity of the universe,
Like the vast blue skies.
That electrical charge
When we made love with our eyes.
Being enveloped by the sun
And gentle breeze that blows
The little cloud of you
That follows wherever I go.
Giving with my heart and soul
For all eternity
And most of all because for ever
I am you and you are me.

INTRODUCTION

For anyone who has ever experienced the magic of true love, that one in a million feeling that you were put on this earth for someone else, destined to spend infinite time with another soul: chances are you probably were.

What can be said about love? It speaks volumes the world over, breaking all language barriers. It has been with us from the beginning of time and will remain for all eternity, a universal code accepted by everyone, and for which there is no substitute. Every day of our lives we hear about it in songs, we see it in plays and television, we read about it in books. We are part of it, yet still we fail to understand. It is my hope that after reading this story there will be a greater understanding.

What can be said about *this* love, a love that stemmed not from aesthetic beauty but from spiritual peace and harmony? Loving someone because of who they are, with all their faults and imperfections, means seeing beyond the exterior, being tuned in to feelings other than your own, loving because you're proud to love.

We are all just pawns in a game of knowledge and truth. Those who play well will receive the highest accolade, but the path of love and life is not an easy one. Many mistakes and pitfalls will be encountered along the way before we earn the right to shed our bodies and propel ourselves into the next dimension.

How do I begin to explain the unexplainable? How do I open the door to a person's mind and make them believe in the unbelievable? I don't know, but I do have the answers to some of life's important questions, and it's these I'd like to share, as I ask you to unlock your minds and open your hearts. By the end of this book you'll think one of two things; that I'm the biggest crackpot that ever walked the earth, or one of the luckiest and most sincere of people; I hope the second.

I begin my turbulent and true account of two lives with Stardust – hopes and dreams – and end with Babylon – absolute, complete, paradise. It is the story of two people who met and fell in love in a place of numbers. It is the story of my life.

As it was in the beginning, is now, and ever shall be.

October 2001

1

First and foremost I'm not a writer, just an ordinary person in an ordinary street in an ordinary town, searching for the words to write an extraordinary story.

The weather is inclement. Remorseless rain is coursing down my sorrow-tainted face. As I gaze across the street my eyes become focussed on the dismal, dreary building opposite. No one could ever have believed, least of all me, that such a humble place would have been chosen for such a special union. Let's take a momentary voyage into the future. Beyond the plain, uninviting doors, a short lifetime of heartache is condensed between four barren walls. Books filled with numbers are everywhere, and the memory of two lovers they brought together. Laughter echoes from an eerie stairwell. Footsteps tread relentlessly, restless spirits still searching, searching, as they pace the empty room. Tears of joy and sadness are branded into the walls; fragments of two souls torn apart by their love for each other.

But in the present it is a place filled with people; hundreds of people who know nothing of the raw emotion once ignited among their surroundings.

I'll take you back to where it all began.

I was born on the 4th December 1964, a minor miracle, as my mother had been told following an earlier operation that she would never have any more children. A very sick baby with double pneumonia and a blood virus, I almost died and was subsequently baptized in hospital. The nurses sat by my incubator and prayed for my survival; I wasn't expected to last the night. God must have been listening. I survived against the odds. Mum told me later how the doctor struggled for several hours to remove the hazardous fluid from my lungs by sucking it into his own mouth, so that I might cry.

From an early age I was treated differently from everyone else; I wasn't sure why. People were nice to me, not because I was a child but because I was me. I knew even then that I'd survived for a reason.

I had an older sister, but there was a fifteen-year age gap between us, and as a result we hardly knew each other. When I was growing up she was away at university. I viewed her as a friend who came to visit at Christmas or birthdays. I felt like an only child. I would spend hours on my own dressing up and play-acting.

Mum worked in a cinema during the evenings, and subsequently at the bingo hall it was converted into; an imposing 1930s building where I spent a great deal of my time as a toddler. Mum didn't like to leave me with a babysitter if Dad was working late, so she took me with her. The manager was a family friend who didn't mind me being there, as long as I stayed out of the way when it got busy. So I would trot around with my cuddly blanket, picking up the used tickets from the floor and playing with them. I had no idea then that they would play such an important part in my life. The bingo concept was a huge success, and the owners subsequently decided to invest in a second property. The new social club across town would incorporate a bingo hall, bowling alley and disco. Mum, being such a long-standing reliable member of staff, was offered the chance of continued employment.

My dad worked during the day for the council, laying footpaths and doing road repairs. Working in the fresh air all day caused him to flake out all evening. He'd spend the best part of it dozing in his chair with the telly on full blast, though he always woke up if I tried to switch it off! As I got older, I grew accustomed to being by myself.

2

We lived in a simple two bedroomed house on a notorious estate. When my parents first moved there, it had been newly-constructed in a desirable area with flower beds on each street corner. Over the years it had deteriorated, and although they contemplated moving many times, something always seemed to stop them.

I was happy living there. Despite its bad reputation, there were many good-hearted people living around us and a lively community spirit. It was near to the town centre, which I could see clearly from my bedroom window, and I loved to sit on my little stool and watch the world go by. There was a large lilac bush just below, and in late spring the wonderful scent would fill the house. The two large trees opposite, richly adorned with delicate pale green foliage, made an interesting landscape throughout the summer months.

Mum cleaned all the time, so home might have been simple but it was well-presented, and Dad liked to grow vegetables in the garden, so we always ate well. I loved all those homely things that make childhood so memorable: The smell of paint at Easter time, of roast dinner on a Sunday, and the shadows created by the sun on the wall at different times throughout the year. Sometimes I was lonely, sometimes I wasn't.

We never had a family holiday, although we did go on day trips, and had lots of fun. Mum was more like a sister to me, as we shared the same interests, and I felt I could talk to her about anything. I was even able to tell her about the special thing I could do when I was five years old.

I had the ability to leave my physical body and move around the room in spirit form. It was something I did frequently, and something which gave me immense pleasure. I could make it happen anywhere in the house, although my most vivid memory is of standing at the top of the stairs. It would begin with a glance in the direction of the rear bedroom. I'd sense an uncomfortable presence in there, something that I had to escape from quickly. Whatever it was it seemed to want me, and simply walking or running down the stairs would not have been fast enough. There was only one way, I concluded, and that was to fly. I knew it was possible, and how to do it. Within seconds I could make it happen.

Concentrating with intensity towards the foot of the stairs, I would begin to lose consciousness. Vision would disappear first, then I'd experience a loud ringing noise in my ears, followed by expulsion from my physical form, when I would feel like a bubble that had burst out from inside myself. Now completely weightless, and able to float around over the bannister, sight and sound would return to me. Enveloped by a powerful feeling of warmth, security and total safety, I was completely invincible. Nothing could touch me now, and on reaching the bottom of the stairs, I could put my feet down and walk or fly around again at will. I was able to dissipate and flatten myself against walls, glide along the ceiling, and observe every tiny flaw in the paintwork with crystal clarity.

If I wanted to return to my physical self I had the power to make it happen just by thinking it. The real me was the being that floated around, not the being I'd left at the top of the stairs; that was just a protective casing, a shell. Once the spirit is outside the body it's just as if there never was a body. It was just something that belonged to me, but it wasn't important. You don't see it. I never looked back on the *physical self*. I knew it was there and how to return to it by working my way back in the relevant direction. It was just instinctive.

At six years old the ability to escape the confines of my body eluded me. However hard I concentrated I just couldn't seem to make it happen any more and I couldn't think why. It had been such a comforting sensation of complete and total freedom, I would miss it terribly. Acceptance was tough on a child of my age who had so easily been able to achieve the unimaginable. This strange insight into another dimension was no longer available to me. I learned to live without it.

My childhood years that followed were pretty ordinary. I loved drama and dancing, both of which I could do well, and dreamed of becoming an actress. Both of these activities allowed me to express myself, and forget my problems. What a fool I could be sometimes.

I don't know whether my sister ever forgave me for the time when her 'boyfriend from hell' made an impromptu visit. I'd been told that should he appear unexpectedly as I played in the front garden one warm, Sunday afternoon, I was to relay the message she was most definitely *not* at home. So when he marched through the gate asking if she was inside, I casually replied 'Yeah, she's sitting in the front room but she told me to tell you she wasn't in.'

'Oh did she now?' came a disgusted reply. 'Thanks very much for that!'

I was only seven years old, the year I wrote my first and only story. I was quite proud of myself when it ended up on display in the school staffroom. But despite my brief literary success I disliked school, and though I tried hard to make friends it was never easy. People seemed to sense that I was different from them, that somehow I didn't belong, and as a result my life was made a misery. Whatever excuse they could come up with they used. I had long blonde hair, wore my uniform, did my homework, carried an umbrella in the rain, (in those days an unforgivable act. Everyone would rather look like drowned rats than be seen carrying a brolly). My defiance was viewed as nonconformity and it became increasingly difficult to escape bullying, both verbal and physical.

My schoolwork suffered. I lost the tiny portion of self-confidence that I had acquired and took consolation in listening to music or watching films of the great love stories like *Wuthering Heights* where I could easily identify with the characters. That mind-blowing, heart-breaking love between Catherine and Heathcliff held a remarkable fascination for me. In sharp contrast I also developed an interest in the occult. I loved to watch horror movies and read books on witchcraft. Thankfully my interest in such matters was short-lived.

When I was 12 mum took me to the new bingo hall, where I could help the cleaners for a couple of pounds' pocket money, and by the grand old age of 14 I'd sometimes be called in to help out if they were short-staffed. This was enjoyable, as I preferred the company of adults to people of my own age, and I got to take part in a variety of interesting jobs. Best of all, I could watch the cabaret at the end of the night. Mostly this was local groups or artistes, but on special occasions we would have famous performers from the 50s or 60s, such as the Platters, or Gerry and the Pacemakers. I was an avid fan of music from this period, particularly the Beatles, and my room was filled with their records, books and posters. Life was pretty good. I was growing up fast and took great interest in the world around me, never more so than in my new place of employment, where curiosity in the supernatural surfaced once again.

Just before I'd started working there, the bowling alley and disco had been removed to make way for extra seating, and the resident ghost who was reputed to haunt the area previously known as 'lane three' was still very much making its presence known. Apparently the hall had been built on the site of an old Roman burial ground, and from the beginning there had been reported incidents of cold spots, people being touched, and even a dog refusing to venture past the point at which lane three began. One customer died of a heart attack in the vicinity of lane three, and new staff members who knew nothing of the ghost story refused to check any winning tickets from customers sitting behind the stage, after feeling a mysterious hand touch them on the shoulder.

One night Mum and I were working near the tele-bingo machines, (for those of you unfamiliar with the term, the ones you find in seaside arcades). I was calling, and Mum had been temporarily enticed away from her main job as head cashier to give out change. There was no one in that part of the building but us and a few customers engrossed in their game. I was desperate for the toilet and the nearest available was in the dressing room at the rear of the stage, so Mum took over my job for a few minutes while I made a quick dash to the pokey unheated little room. All was quiet but for the sound of Mum's clear soft speech in the background and the noise of plastic shutters sliding across machines. I didn't lock myself in, just closed the door behind me, but when I tried to get out it appeared to be stuck rigid, apparently held from the opposite side. I pulled and pulled, with such force I tore my finger. Eventually Mum came looking for me and I called out in panic 'The door won't open. I'm trapped.' Mum gently pushed the door and it swung effortlessly inwards.

It was a mysterious place; when the last of the mighty crowds had finally left for home and the last light had been switched off; it always seemed rather eerie and cold.

2

I was fast approaching 16. It was the aptly-named era of the 'New Romantics' and my life was about to change beyond my wildest dreams. After some months' absence working elsewhere, Mum and I had returned to work at the bingo hall. On our first night back it wasn't the supernatural aura that held my attention. It was a new member of staff, and I spent the best part of the evening engrossed in detailed observation of his every move. He was different from the others, and stood out from the crowd with his slim build, dark hair, glasses and cheeky grin. He seemed to move so quickly with a determined spring in his step. If you were to blink you might miss him. Suddenly our eyes locked with a strange familiarity. It was almost as if we already knew each other, but we'd never met before. He stopped dead in his tracks, completely and utterly spellbound by my presence, as I was by his. He made numerous attempts to get on with his work, despite being repeatedly side-tracked by my inquisitive eyes. No one had ever looked at me with such fondness before nor, I suspect, at him, and I suddenly stood tall with pride and significance. He was intriguing. Who was this person with whom I shared such an affinity, and who commanded my undivided attention? I found myself seized with curiosity.

He breezed up to me and placed his arm affectionately around my shoulder. His energy hit me like a bolt of lightning.

'Hi, I'm John. You used to work here before, didn't you?'

'Yes;' I replied suspiciously. 'How did you know that?'

'I just do. You know this is amazing. I can't believe it. It's you, it's *Really* you!'

'*And* you,' I replied.

For a few magical seconds, we seemed to have become lost in another world. What were we talking about?

I felt decidedly comfortable and relaxed in his company. I could talk to him about anything, and he quickly became my best friend. We had three things in common, and that was probably about all, as we shared none of the same interests. We were the same birth-sign, were the same height, and we both wore glasses. There was one year between us in age (he was older); like me was still at school during the day, and lived in the only other residential area of the town as bad as mine. There was nothing more than friend-ship and fun between us, though it soon became obvious to the others we shared a unique bond.

Night after night I watched him hug each member of staff as I waited patiently for my turn. I always seemed to get more than anyone else. He found me attractive, as I did him in a strange sort of way, and my heart would race feverishly whenever he came near. I found myself thrilled and excited by his attentions.

Yet despite the fact that my emotions were spiralling out of control, I had eyes for someone else. I'd taken a fancy to a boy who worked on the tills in Sainsbury's supermarket, so I made a point of going in every Saturday to buy a load of groceries I didn't really need, in the hope that he might ask me out. Eventually, after several weeks of eye-contact and flirting, he did. He was good-looking in an unconventional way. It boosted my confidence and I revelled in telling John all about the latest object of my desire. He was my best friend after all, and I valued his advice; with the added bonus of fuelling a little jealousy.

Mathew, the boy from Sainsburys, and I went out together for a while. He'd had quite a few sexual conquests before me, so was able to teach me a thing or two about life.

Over the weeks we enjoyed several romantic encounters, including one particularly memorable day in a cornfield. Then he dumped me in order to be reconciled with his former girlfriend, a dark-haired South American beauty. I was upset at first, but

Mathew opened my eyes to many things. He told me that the world was my oyster, my mum was my best friend, and that love and life were waiting for me. After my brief yet enlightening time with him, I felt wiser, sexually more mature, and keen to put my new-found knowledge into practice.

Once or twice a week our neighbours would have a CB-radio meeting at their house, creating an influx of unconventional strangers with vehicles to match. One visitor held my attention. Tall, dark and for want of a better word, smarmy. Just the sort of person that an impressionable teenage girl might find desirable. He'd shuffle down the path in his suede shoes, stare up at my bedroom window, then beckon me down to join him. I always resisted, until after making some discreet enquiries regarding his marital status, I managed to get myself invited round for the next meeting. I had quite a crush on him for a while, until I discovered that he was, after all, married and did this sort of thing on a regular basis.

John showered me with sympathy after I'd made a fool of myself once again. 'It's not your fault,' he said. 'You've just been choosing all the wrong people.' In the locality of mysterious lane three he'd chat me up each night with exaggerated promises of sexual heaven. With a comforting hug around my shoulders he'd say 'I don't know why you bother with them when you could have me!'

'Well then, why don't you show me what you've got to offer?'

'I will then. Meet me after work.'

'OK, after work then.'

'You just don't know what you're missing.'

I would complain regularly about wanting Saturday night off, and how the management always refused to let me have it.

'I'd let you have it,' John would respond eagerly.

'Would you really? That's nice.'

'Yeah, and the night off!'

I was fascinated by his brash crudity and charming smile. Sexual banter like this characterized our every exchange.

'Right, after work then, yeah?'

'Yeah, I'll show you a really good time.'

'No, I'll show *you* a good time.' Then in a barely audible whisper he added a much cruder suggestion. Did he really have the audacity to say what I just thought he said? I couldn't quite believe my ears.

'*What* was that?'

With startled eyes and an innocent expression he'd stare back at me and say, 'Me? Me? Didn't say anything!'

The idea that we might get together at the end of our night's work for a passion-filled assignation was just a joke, yet highly stimulating. No one had ever shown such profound interest in me before. Really, we were both far too nervous to put it to the test, and after the last session finished we'd just return to our respective houses.

But each night our conversation, fuelled with promiscuous undertones, intensified. As soon as I arrived I couldn't wait to tease him.

'So where were you last night? I waited specially but you didn't come!'

With a perplexed expression he'd stare at his trousers. 'How did you know?'

'You really have got a disgusting mind,' I'd tell him.

'So have you. Anyway it was me who waited for you and you didn't come. Missed the chance now. Could have been so good!'

'Well,' I'd say teasingly, 'we could always make it tonight.'

'OK then. You better not let me down. You better turn up this time.'

'I will.'

Our eyes locked in wanton lust. As the evening progressed he'd brush past me and whisper, 'I hope you're ready for it. I can't wait.'

The tickets that were sold for the last game of the night were called 'big-enders'. At the same time every evening a couple of old Scottish ladies would hobble in; when John and I were serving

11

one would shout to the other, 'It's all right Maisie, it's John tonight; John will have a big-ender for us, won' t you son? He's a good boy!'

'Didn't think it showed,' he'd mutter cheekily.

'Pardon son? What did you say?'

'Me? Nothing, nothing.'

Maisie had an eye-patch, a walking stick and her grey hair was a mass of greasy ringlets. The look of anticipation on her face as she waited for John to present her with his big-ender made me dive swiftly beneath the counter to snigger safely in private.

'There's only one left, I'm afraid,' I heard him reply.

'Thank you son,' Maisie's friend would reply. 'You can have John's big-ender tonight, Maisie, and I'll manage without it, or we can share it if you like.' I tried hard not to wet myself.

Time and again we ignited our feelings with such erotic innuendo, but I don't believe either of us felt for one minute it would lead anywhere. Weeks and weeks would pass by, each night beginning with the same arrangement, a secret meeting after work that would never materialize. I'd check the winning ticket, then approach John with the customer's membership number in order to collect the prize money from, him.

'Come on, John! Give it to me,' I'd instruct.

'What here? Now? OK then!' he'd reply excitedly. Our bodies had yet to enjoy intimacy, but our eyes had been making love since that first night.

Then I became ill with flu. Unable to raise myself from bed I decided to stay off work for a couple of days. When Mum returned the first night, she said that John had enquired about me, and asked if he could come and visit the following evening. She'd told him he could. 'I hope you don't mind,' she said.

Actually I did mind. I was slightly annoyed with her for not consulting me first. John and I were close, and I was fond of him, but having him come up to my room and see me in bed, after all the smutty suggestions we'd been making to each other for weeks, was just a bit too close for comfort. I'd never thought seriously about taking things any further with him. I didn't fancy him in the way that you usually fancy someone, because of the way they look, but I was drawn to his personality, and my stomach did seem to react in a strange way whenever he approached me or entered the room.

The following evening, he arrived as arranged, with a box of chocolates in hand, the nicest chocolates I'd ever tasted.

'Hurry up and get well soon,' he said. 'Work just isn't the same without you there.'

'Really? That's a nice thing to say.'

'It's true. I'm missing you.'

We talked for a while, listened to some music (New Romantic, of course), and his presence that night left me feeling comfortable and contented in a way I couldn't describe.

When I did return, things seemed somehow different. Our friendship continued to blossom, and the sexual innuendo flourished throughout every conversation, but the jovial undercurrent was replaced by something far more serious. What had started out as teenage promiscuous banter and messing around, had now turned into a genuine desire for closeness.

It was far past time that we put our words into actions. Things had gone on too long. This time we would follow it through, so we made arrangements for a rendezvous at John's house after our shift had finished.

John was one of six children from a Catholic family, so we were lucky that his parents and most of his brothers and sisters were in bed, with the exception of one, who was still in the living room watching television. John gave him some money to leave us alone. I can't remember why that room was chosen as opposed to the bedroom, but nevertheless, the scene was set. I'd spent most of the day in a state of anxiety and panic over the outcome of tonights long awaited tryst, and now suddenly it was upon me.

We sat down on the sofa and deliberated over which one of us was going to make the first move. I leaned forward and kissed him in an effort to break the ice. It didn't even crack. He remained tense and uncomfortable.

'I've never kissed anyone before' he said. 'I don't know how to do it. I don't know how to be.'

I kissed him again. This time with a little more depth and persuasion.

'It's all right,' I said. 'It doesn't matter. You'll find your own way and it'll be perfect. Just do what comes naturally. There's no right or wrong way. Just be yourself. So I take it you've never...?'

'No. I've never done anything like this before,' he replied nervously. 'You must be very disappointed.'

'No. Not at all,' I answered. 'Well then, looks like I'm going to make love to you!' His eyes lit up like a freshly-struck match.

After all the weeks of bragging, I was determined to make a memorable, lasting impression. I suddenly realized I had this power over him: his first sexual encounter, something that he would remember all his life, was in my gift. I had put on some stockings for the big event, and I think now I must have frightened him to death. This poor boy had never even kissed anyone before, and was about to be seduced. I had read quite a bit of a book on 'sexual techniques', though I was hardly qualified in the art of ravishing young Catholics. First time for everything, I thought!

Very provocatively, I began to remove some of my clothing, then I began on his. The freshly-struck-match look had now been replaced by that of a rabbit caught in headlights, prior to being crushed. 'Try to relax,' I whispered.

I let him feel the warmth of my lips on his naked skin, then continued my arousal technique with an enthusiastic tongue, tantalizing him further with a sweep of my long hair as it cascaded over my tense shoulders. Underwear removed, I hitched up my skirt to reveal my most intimate secret between stocking-fringed thighs. I slithered down onto his body, observing the look of pleasurable surprise that unfolded across his face with every thrusting movement. Our eyes remained fixed, each on the other. My hot, rampant breasts glided softly over the contours of his cheekbones and rested firmly on his lips. They parted momentarily allowing my nipple to enter. He absorbed it readily

14

and began to suck. I enticed him with every gentle brush of my craving flesh, as I pushed my womanly curves into his slender adolescent form. 'Is it enjoyable for you?' I asked, rather stupidly, knowing full well he was in no position to answer. With a mumble, a nod and a giggle he confirmed what his expressions had already conveyed.

It was a mutually delightful experience that left us both with a sense of inner peace and tranquillity. We'd spent so long wondering what it would be like with each other; now at last we knew.

Afterwards he took comfort in playing with my hair, tangled and sweaty though it was. His eyes were brimming with adoration and bewilderment.

'Was I OK?' he asked nervously.

'Perfect,' I replied, 'just perfect.'

'You know' he said, 'when you left the bingo hall, I was employed as your replacement. Don't you think that's strange?'

'So that's how you knew I'd worked there before?'

'Yes. If you hadn't left I would never have got that job, and we would never have met, but I did and you came back, just like it was meant to happen that way.'

'I suppose it is strange isn't it? Fate, probably,' I replied with a tender kiss, my body still perspiring and faintly throbbing with excitement.

3

I continued to value our unique friendship, and the extraordinary sense of peace and tranquillity I felt when we were alone together, and I did love him, but I couldn't say I was in love with him at that time. But John became infatuated with me after our night of passion, and I wasn't sure if I could feel the same way about him. The longer I let things continue, the more complex our lives would become. Everything seemed to be moving so fast. I had no control over my emotions. I had to put an end to the more serious side of our relationship. It wasn't fair to lead him on and give him false hopes. I knew he'd be devastated, so I put it off for as long as possible, and watched with trepidation as he fell deeper and deeper in love with me. My mind was jumbled. I craved some time and space to make sense of what was happening.

One night in my kitchen, just after we d finished clearing away the dishes from our supper, I told him it was over. With an incredulous stare, through tear-filled eyes, he asked me what he'd done wrong. I tried to explain as best I could, that he hadn't done anything wrong, I just needed to sort out my feelings. I told him I'd like us to remain friends, and for now that was all I could offer. Maybe in the future it would be different. He looked so sad and empty. I felt dreadful. He wanted much more from me than just friendship. Until then we'd shared an enjoyable evening, and now my heartless actions had left him feeling deflated and worthless. The disappointment and rejection that engulfed every feature was heart-rending to me. I wanted to ease the pain, retract those last few words. He'd been so good, compassionate and loving. He really didn't deserve any of this. His vulnerability melted my heart. I was touched by his warmth and sensitivity, and the fact that he was able to cry openly without fear of ridicule.

I watched him walk away, still fighting back the tears as they tumbled down his cheeks, sickened by my own actions, yet at the same time free of the weight that I had been bearing on my shoulders for weeks.

'Don't you feel guilty?' Mum asked. 'You've been rotten to that poor boy and he thinks the world of you.'

Yes, I did feel guilty, but I also felt I'd done what I had to do. It was over and done with now.

Our friendship did continue and surprisingly so did the flirting. I would obtain a strange satisfaction from the glint of jealousy in his eyes when I passed comment on men I found attractive. Even though I'd made my feelings crystal-clear, I still desired John's attentions, and he wasn't about to give up on me.

The staff Christmas party was upon us before we knew it, and I was eager to look my very best. For the occasion I'd purchased a virtually non-existent mini-dress with gold belt, gold shoes, and I had mum weave some gold ribbon through my hair.

The party wouldn't begin till the bingo had finished, so we had to work all night dressed in our finest. Everyone commented on how nice I looked, but strangely it was still John's attentions I craved above all others'. Several times during the course of the evening he glanced hopefully in my direction. I knew he still wanted me, and his eyes so filled with desire propelled me to the highest peak of arousal.

Before making our way next door to the club where the party was to be held, we jumped up onto the counter and swung our legs back and forth in childish unison while we waited impatiently for the others to join us.

Louise, one of our colleagues stood chatting to a man I had difficulty averting my gaze from. Upon his leaving I jumped in with both feet.

'Who was that?' I asked inquisitively.

'That was *my* boyfriend,' she replied with a cocky smile.

'He's gorgeous.'

'Do you fancy him then?'

'Well, put it this way, I wouldn't say no if you decided to throw him in my direction!'

With every word uttered I could observe the resentment building in John's eyes, though he was trying hard to keep it from view. As it increased, so did my passion.

'Come on, John, let's go!' I hugged him affectionately, in a kind of sisterly fashion, then took hold of his hand ready to whisk him away. For a few seconds our eyes became locked and a syrupy-sweet, icing sugar smile was exchanged between us. I dragged him through the nearest entrance door, then promptly left him on arrival at the bar, in order to find Mum's table.

'Love the blouse!' shouted Tom, the club manager. 'Pity you've forgotten your skirt!'

'Oh, very funny', I replied. 'Very droll!' John smiled, and some of the girls began to gather round. Being his usual charming self, he placed his arms firmly around their shoulders. One or two of them were flirting with him and he revelled in their smiles and fleeting touches. I hated it. They had no right to touch him. He had no right to touch them. He was *mine*! He belonged to *me*! God, what was I thinking? I'd been the one to put an end to any romantic involvement between the two of us, so why was I now feeling so incredibly jealous?

Before long he appeared at our table. 'Can I get you some more drinks?' he asked.

'Thank you,' I replied. 'That would be nice.'

After he'd returned to the bar, Mum leaned across the table and began to whisper in my ear. She must have perceived the envy in my gaze. 'You know he really is a lovely boy. Why don't you give him another chance?'

'Do you think I should?' I eagerly awaited her confirmation.

'Yes. I do. Go on, what are you waiting for? There aren't many around who are as sincere as him, you know.'

Perhaps she was right. If I were to leave it much longer, he'd be snapped up by someone else, then I'd be kicking myself for waiting so long. What was I to do? I was still wrestling with my conscience when suddenly a loud thud of glasses on the table brought me back to reality. With a warm smile, he sat down beside me and began to run his fingers through my hair. I hadn't said that he could, but strangely he seemed to sense that I wanted it.

'All right then?' he asked.

That's when it hit me: A touch that left me spellbound, and a look of love that left me paralysed with delight; the moment when I knew for the first time *he* was the one. I stood at love's precipice ready and waiting to fall right in. His eyes captured my attention. I became aware of a perceptible change in their appearance. What to my observation before had just been an ordinary pair of eyes much like anyone else's, had now become full of mystery, full of adoration for me, and the most striking shade of blue. I reciprocated, and let my fingers slide over his dark, silken locks. I remembered how sensually his body had glided between my thighs.

'Let's give it another try,' I whispered. 'Do you still want to?'

'Yes,' he answered. 'You've made me so happy.'

We kissed tenderly, and I seemed to sense from that very moment that nothing could ever come between us.

4

From that day on we would become inseparable, going everywhere together hand in hand, or arm in arm. I was so proud I
wanted to shout out to everyone, 'Look who *I've* got!' I felt so
lucky. What an idiot I'd been to ever dream of ending it all in the
first place!

We couldn't bear to be apart even for short periods of time.
Without each other's company we were lost. Whenever he left the
room he seemed to take part of me with him. I'd walk through
the town feeling alone when suddenly he'd swoop up behind
me and give me the biggest kiss, charging me up with a pulsating,
dynamic current of emotion. That boundless energy and fascinating
magnetism would be transferred from his lips to mine with
irrefutable certainty. I never believed that love could be this good. I
couldn't eat, I couldn't sleep, I could think of nothing but him and
how good he made me feel. It was a time of utter bliss and
contentment. A beautiful but turbulent time that would change our
lives forever.

The sex was amazing. It just got better and better. All the
right moves came naturally. It wasn't something that could be
learned by reading a book, I discovered, it was all about wanting
to try as many nice things as possible to please the other, and
finding different ways to show how much we loved. We enjoyed
learning together. John's awkwardness faded with time and
he discovered how to relax more, taking pleasure in my body.
One night we'd been wrestling playfully on the sofa when
suddenly we were interrupted by a familiar television advert. (The

one where a certain chocolate bar is just enough for a special treat).

'Now that gives me an idea!' I giggled.

'I haven't got one of those,' John replied disappointedly.

'I have a Cadbury's flake though.'

He slipped it seductively between my legs. His lustful eyes impaled themselves on mine. My heart fluttered as he pleasured me. Minutes later I watched him take it into his mouth. The now moist, velvety crumbling chocolate revealing that ever so secretive little hint of me.

'That's the best flake I ever had,' he whispered.

'For me too,' I sighed.

We laughed, he kissed me, and we made love.

Others found it difficult to accept our close relationship.

'Oh here comes John and his shadow,' they'd quip nastily, or 'He can't even go to the toilet without her following behind!' If I did follow him to the toilet, it was because I harboured an ulterior motive, and it usually paid off! The more love and affection he bestowed the more I craved, and the happier we became the more it unnerved those around us. We were seen as a joke because we were so different from one another. John was casual and carefree, I was prim and proper. I saw danger in everything, he feared nothing. Like chalk and cheese, it was said; we were exact opposites.

His exceptional disposition made it impossible for anyone to view him other than admirably. Always ready to help if there was a problem, he was a great listener. Nothing was too much trouble no matter how inconvenient, and his hugs lifted you from despondency to delight in seconds. Like a ray of sunshine, he brought light and joy into everyone's world, especially mine.

He loved football, Duran Duran, Madness and hard work. He was the only person I have ever known to work every day of his fortnight's summer holiday each year because he didn't like to let anyone down if they needed him. I was attracted to all these remarkable qualities, but particularly his sense of humour, which mirrored my own. He could make me laugh as no one else on earth could. Our newly-created world was an amalgamation of giggles, childish pranks and most importantly, love.

The month of January saw the annual haggis-eating championship at the bingo hall take place. First the enormous plate of stodge would be carried down the gangway by a twirling kilt-bedecked numpty, to the sound of 'Windy Miller' on the bagpipes and the recitation of Rabbie Burns's famous poem. Then the towns most gluttonous men would assemble in line on the stage, and shovel a full five pounds of lukewarm entrails into their mouths, seemingly without any prior insight that their following hours would be spent in the toilets endeavouring to bring it all back up again. As if the whole event wasn't stomach-churning enough, we all had to dress like silver service waiters in black and white for the entire evening, and suffer the indignity of appearing to the rest of the country via the evening news as though it was something to be proud of.

There was usually enough of a furore to slip away for a few minutes and steal a kiss, or perhaps something more. John would clear the machine, switch off the caller's mike and entice me away to the nearest available undisturbed room. Distant sounds of clapping and cheering at the contest could almost have been in response to our union, as we devoured each other's bodies without restraint. We would creep out innocently afterwards to a sea of inquisitive eyes.

'You've left your balls out, John!' someone sneered.

'Can't say I noticed!' he replied with a startled expression downwards and a massive grin. They were referring to the ones on the stage, which he'd left absent mindedly on top of the machine.

I felt so completely at ease in his company, I couldn't wait to go into work each night just to see him; it was the only thing I looked forward to all day. I found pleasure in dressing up and making up. I craved his attention more than anything, and the more effort I put in the more he began to take notice; in fact everyone began to notice.

I'd stand patiently in the aisle waiting for the sudden hush which swept the sound of gossip from the air, as John prepared to call the first number of the night. As his voice echoed from wall to wall I found myself captivated once again by his every move, mesmerized for the following 40 minutes or so till the interval. We were starstruck young lovers, the epitome of everything loyal and true. Surrounded by constant pandemonium between sessions, our typical night consisted of head-jarring sounds: the incessant, mindless chatter of hundreds of voices and different accents, the shower of clanking, jangling twenty-pence pieces falling into wooden money drawers, and paper money flapping in the air like little seaside flags. I would put on a money bag and tear around subjecting myself to innumerable hands thumping my arm or prodding my back through a cloudy haze of cigarette smoke, as I dished out change faster than a fruit machine.

Pompous Peter Kingston stands eagerly awaiting a 'granny stampede' on the change drawer in his best bib and tucker, complete with dickie-bow, his bald head shinier than the piles of new coins arranged meticulously in front of him. 'I do believe I feel quite dizzy,' he groans, as a deluge of hands start throwing ten- and twenty-pound notes in every direction. Above the racket our two pairs of eyes scrutinize and summon. The bell has just sounded: The nine o'clock session will commence shortly. The masses return to their seats on cue, grappling with their winnings and fumbling with their purses, unaware that the two pairs of eyes behind them are engaging in spiritual intercourse.

When the games have all finished and the crowd has dispersed, Robert searches for John with the offer of overtime behind the bar. Our time is so precious we need to spend as much as we can together, so we take off at speed, downstairs to the room that stores the tickets. Giggling like a couple of naughty schoolchildren we listen to Robert's raised voice and heavy footsteps as he makes his tireless search throughout the building.

'John, where the hell are you?' He must have heard our giggling. 'You're down in that bloody book room, aren't you? Get up here right now this minute! Do you hear me?'

We kiss nervously, lips trembling with excitement. 'Mmm, that's nice,' John mumbles, then shouts at the top of his voice, 'I'm just COMING, Robert!'

'You mucky little bugger! Get up here now!'

All we'd shared was a kiss, but that incident instigated all the 'book room' rumours. We decided to fuel them with some truth, and each lovemaking session that followed was more stimulating than the last. We'd sell the tickets afterwards in the knowledge that the customers would be mortified if they knew where their books had been and what a story they could tell. We managed not to get caught.

Valentine's day was approaching and I looked forward to it with optimistic expectation. I'd always been the one at school who never got any cards. This year I had the feeling my luck was about to change. That morning I opened the door to a beautiful bouquet of flowers, and later John gave me a card. Inside he'd written down the words of a song, words that came straight from the heart. So very typical, so incredibly romantic. I was happier then than I ever believed possible. I loved everything about him from his swift movements to his razor-sharp wit.

His twisted sense of humour remained a constant source of fascination to me. Customers were always giving him presents and wishing him 'Happy Birthday' at different times throughout the year, and this would baffle everyone.

'It can't be your birthday again!' Robert would say suspiciously. 'You had one only last month!'

'So? I decided to have another one this month!' John would reply cheekily.

'Yeah, why do people keep giving you presents when it's not your birthday?' I'd ask inquisitively.

'If people want to give me presents because they think it's my birthday, who am I to argue?' he'd respond with a devilish sparkle about the eyes.

He had a great love of people, enjoyed humouring them and

tried to understand the more profound aspects of their personalities. Others' lives were greatly enriched just by knowing him. He could get them to open up, to let him peruse their inner psyche. When entering a room, he brought with him a mysterious aura; it glowed like a warm veil of spring sunshine and everyone would immediately notice he'd entered. He'd spend much time after work sitting by the bar with me and some of the other female staff members, listening intently to their tales of childbirth. During the conversation he'd nod understandingly, then glance at me with a perplexed expression as if to say, 'What the hell am I doing here? What do I know about having babies?' He might not have known about pregnancy and birth, but he knew all about tuning himself in to others' feelings, particularly mine. The customers shared as much of an affinity with him as the staff.

'Get me a budgie, John!' One old lady would demand each afternoon. We all knew she wasn't quite the full ticket. 'Stupid old bag!' Robert would mutter under his breath.

That she may have been, but John would tilt his head to one side, cuddle her tightly and with a smile that could melt ice reply, 'I will get you a budgie! Don't worry, I will get you a budgie!'

I'd look on with admiration and think to myself how I wished I could be more like that.

It was a mad world we found ourselves in, rather like being in a soap opera. Everyone was at it with someone. The barmaid was carrying on with the cellar man, in the cellar; the director with the supervisor. When he breezed in late every Tuesday night, her evening off singing 'Suspicious Minds', we all knew where he'd spent the last few hours and with whom. There were those who were always ready for a fumble with the bouncers from the club next door. In the middle of it all, John and I were simply in love, 'truly, madly, deeply'. I would spend every spare minute singing Cilla Black's 'You're My World' while gazing in John's direction, and he would try to make me giggle as I called tele-bingo numbers, in the interval by seductively eating a banana.

'Absolutely disgusting!' someone would shout between games.

25

'I thought it was rather nice actually.' John would mumble. '*And the banana!*' Causing me to smirk like a halfwit, as I tried with little success to keep suitable control.

We all got on so well, like one big family; we moaned about the job, of course, but were always able to share a joke. When the last of the customers had vacated the premises, we would congregate down by the bar and drink, or even play our own game of staff bingo. Whoever got the short straw had to call. Sometimes after the director had gone home for the evening we would order a group curry and eat it in the office. He couldn't stand the smell of Indian food so this was strictly forbidden, though it was not unknown for him to return later on while we were still eating it. His commanding voice could be heard in the distance, and shaking with fear we'd try to hide the evidence under the desk in the bin. The office door would swing violently open and in he would march with that steely look. Tall and stern, wearing his one and only blue suit, the one he lived in night after night. We called him Hissing Sid, because of his bad-tempered outbursts and constant snarling. The smell of curry would be plainly detectable.

'I hope that's not bloody curry I can smell in here!' he'd shout angrily.

'No!' we'd all roar back in unison. 'No one's had any curry in here!'

'Good then, because if I come in here tomorrow and find anything in the bin to suggest otherwise, you're all bloody sacked!'

Afterwards, when cashing up, we would listen to the music pounding through the wall from the nightclub next door. Many a night I danced around the cash desk to the sound of Dexy's Midnight Runners while I waited for John to dash around the hall and switch off the main lights and machines. Meanwhile, the phone would ring. It was our regular pervert who wanted to know what colour knickers we were wearing. We all humoured him, and would gather round the phone giggling.

'We'll tell you what colour we've got on, if you tell us what you're wearing.'

'Red satin ones tonight,' came a soft-spoken reply.

Eventually Suzanne would grab the phone. 'I'm not telling you again – piss off, you dirty pervert!' He usually left it for a couple of days, but could be relied upon to call again.

As for the customers, half of them were mad as hatters. Some were nasty, but there were the special few that made it all worthwhile. One of our favourites was a postman whom we called 'Jeeves' because he spoke with such a posh accent. Every Thursday night he would make his dramatic entrance and shout over to Mum in the cash desk, 'Evening, Mater!' Then approaching John and me on the ticket counter: 'Wow you look absolutely ravishing tonight, doesn't she, John? You lucky devil, you!'

'I know I am,' he'd reply, with his hand up the back of my skirt.

'If only I were twenty years younger!' Jeeves would continue as he stared at my provocative black lace top. 'Love the blouse. Sensational! I bet Mater doesn't approve. I say Mater,' he'd shout. 'Bet you don't approve of the blouse, what?'

'No!' Mum would yell back, 'definitely not!'

'Well, it's made my evening, I can tell you.'

Another favourite customer was Vic. With the cheekiest smile you ever saw, and a mischievous twinkle in his eyes, he would repeat the same question night after night: 'When's the big day, then? I don't want to miss it, you know. Pair of love-birds like you two – it'll really be something special.'

'Ah, that would be telling. Give us time,' we'd reply.

'I better get that invite. Don't forget, I want it by the end of the week.'

'No, we won't forget.'

'Seriously, you make a lovely couple. As soon as I get my invite, I'll say no more on the subject.'

I did want to marry John, but I wondered if our big day would ever come; something made me think it wouldn't. Yet we were so tuned in to one another, it seemed the most natural thing on earth to spend the rest of our lives together. There was that certain way he looked at me sometimes, so that I could almost pick up his thoughts. I'd stare back at him with spellbound eyes and say to myself; 'I know exactly what you're thinking. Whatever it is you and I are made of; it's the same.' Now and again our minds were in complete unison, and it was a magical feeling. It was a compelling attraction, and one which we had to act upon. Often we'd be overpowered by an insatiable need for further intimacy.

A typical evening would see us sit down to a shared take-away, listen to some music or make a half-hearted attempt at watching a film in between bouts of lovemaking. Then we would fall asleep in each other's arms, only to wake at around 3 a.m. with the sobering thought that John still had to walk me home, and I still had to find a way of creeping in without being heard. Unfortunately for me I usually was. It was those romantic walks home that bring back my happiest memories. In the cold autumn winds I would be unaware of my feet making contact with the ground, except for the sound of rustling leaves beneath them. When they were sore and blistered from ridiculously-styled, ill-fitting shoes, he'd sweep me up and carry me the rest of the way.

Then there was that moment of waking from our warm peaceful sleep to the sight of swirling snowflakes as they spiralled towards the ground beyond the window pane. We'd be only too aware that it was bitterly cold out there and we had to find some energy to get dressed, go out again and brave the weather. We'd shake and shiver as we left the warm haven of bed, and braced ourselves for the impending journey, and that first freezing droplet of cold air on our heated young bodies.

Not a sound could be heard, save for our feet crunching through the blanket of white ice. Our lips touched, my arms held him close, his held me closer, and God's arms embraced us both. I'd arrive home looking like the abominable snowman, but with contented soul and happy heart.

In our times alone, we would listen to the love songs that John Lennon had written for Yoko Ono. We were fascinated by their relationship; they were torn apart by criticism of those who didn't understand that need to be with another person 24 hours a day, which to most people is incomprehensible and obsessive. We knew that kind of love; it wasn't alien to us. It was here and now, and for always. We would make love to the music of the 'Double Fantasy' album, sharing in their unity and their peace.

In our work, John continued to make me laugh at every opportunity. One night, I was calling the main session on stage. It was the busiest part of the evening, and the hall was filled from end to end. John was checking. He'd been up to his usual tricks, mouthing obscenities and making seductive suggestions, then hiding behind the clipboard that held the prize-money envelopes. I was driven to distraction by the alluring way in which he would lick them before sealing the contents securely in.

There was a deathly silence, as hundreds of ears were pricked in anticipation of the following number. I called it. Suddenly, there was a tremendous roar of shouting. I'd already called that number earlier in the game. It meant checking every one, in order to find my mistake. This time they were forgiving. Next time they weren't. Someone put their hand into the air, but I failed to notice. I had already begun to call the next number. Once you've done that, there's no way back; the caller's decision is final. John stared at me with dread as half the customers began screaming and threatening me. Then Hissing Sid appeared at the rear of the hall, waving his arms and indicating that the game must resume. Fortunately everyone simmered down by the time the next house had been won.

Heaven knows what the customers made of us, though most understood our feelings. We couldn't stop touching and we couldn't stop loving. We flirted and groped and kissed behind the stage during the course of the evening's work, and whenever we thought no one was looking; I couldn't wait for the thrill of his lustful body pushing hard against mine, a whiff of aftershave, and a sweep of silken hair against my ear. Fragile, willowy fingers beneath my skirt, stroking my thighs and massaging my hips, or a soothing kiss on my feverish breast, passionate clinches whenever

29

a spare moment could be grasped. Sometimes, we would be caught. The nice customers joked about it and were happy for us, but some of them threatened to report us to the management for not taking our work seriously, in which case we'd try desperately hard to behave until we'd finished for the night.

We were reported once, and Robert told John to collect his cards at the end of his shift. John said his Mum would be furious if he went home and told her he'd lost his job. How could he sack him? I was so angry, I insisted that if John left, I'd follow on principle. After we had spent several hours in a state of panic and upset, Robert confessed he'd just been winding us up. John was far too good a worker; there was never any question of letting him go. He just wanted to make us sweat for a bit, and to realize that we should perhaps tone down our feelings for each other during working hours.

Mum kept a watchful eye on us both. She enjoyed playing the part of the possessive mother, who would protect her daughter at any cost. When we clocked off for the night, she'd say in a posh, stern voice: 'I hope you're not going to corrupt my daughter?'

John would reply with mock outrage. 'Me? Me corrupt her! I was sweet and innocent till I met her!'

'What did you say?' Mum would snap back.

John would cough sarcastically. He knew the real me.

'Leave them alone you old bag and let them enjoy themselves,' Robert would butt in.

'Yeah that's right, Griselda.'

'How dare you call me Griselda?' Mum would scream in rage.

'If you don't behave yourself. I'll put a curse on you!'

He'd duck down sharply and roll his eyes towards the ceiling in fearful anticipation.

'Get up you fool,' I'd say.

'She might hit me with her broomstick.'

'You make sure you have her at home by 1 a.m.,' Mum would add insistently. (He'd take hold of my hand in preparation for a swift exit).

'Don't worry, I'll HAVE her at your house before midnight. I'll look forward to that!'

Heads turned and conversation ceased, as we charged through the office door and down those steps gripping each other so tightly we were practically flying. It seemed that the world had suddenly stopped to listen and to watch. The night was ours for the taking.

5

Life was wonderful. I was in a state of permanent elation. Whether we made love, kissed or just held each other, there was the most perfect feeling of peace and completeness. Yet my exuberance was always tainted by a glimmer of despair. Niggling voices inside my head could not be silenced. *This happiness wasn't meant for this life; not for this life!* What we had was too good. We seemed to know instinctively that it couldn't last.

Then there was the evening when a tip-off from a local prison indicated that we might be raided by some unsavoury characters with sawn-off shotguns. I had the nerve-racking job of being on the door that night, flanked by police officers who remained firmly out of sight behind a wooden partition. The atmosphere was incredibly tense. We'd been told not to put our lives at risk should we be threatened. Mum was under no obligation to fulfil her usual duties in the cash desk, though she decided to remain. We all put on a very brave front, and in answer to our prayers, the evening passed without any hitches.

Our regular doorman was rather elderly, and it was decided after this that a younger man would be more appropriate under the circumstances. So Nathan made his debut, who thought himself God's gift to women. Most of us just thought he was a prat, except for Gwen, the cashier who fancied him like mad. She was married to Harvey, a man more than twice her age, but being married never stopped anyone before, and they embarked upon a passionate affair.

One night after work, things came to a climax. We were, as

usual, all down by the bar when the stage telephone rang. Who could it be so late at night? Mum tiptoed onto the platform and picked it up. We were all mouthing, who is it? We watched in astonishment as she carefully placed the receiver back without uttering a single word.

'It was Harvey;' she replied, 'asking if Gwen was still here. I didn't know what to say.'

'Bloody hell,' said Gwen. 'Did he sound angry?'

'I don't know, I didn't wait to find out.'

On our way home we bumped into the man himself.

'Where's my Gwen? Is she in there?' he shouted,with a face like thunder. 'I know she is!' He pushed past us and marched through the club. Not surprisingly the evening's antics, and the affair, ended with a showdown and a car chase through the town centre. I wasn't too sure whether I'd made the right decision in leaving early. Seems I'd missed all the excitement.

In pursuit of some relaxation after these events, I decided on a day-trip to London. Four of us would travel down by coach, and do our own thing once we'd arrived: John, Cathy, Mum and me.

It was a beautiful morning. The sky was blue and the birds were singing; it was just perfect, until John failed to get on at the designated stop. I couldn't believe he hadn't showed. I was left annoyed and angry, as my plans for a romantic day had suddenly gone straight out of the bus window.

On arrival, Cathy took off on her own while Mum and I stayed together on Oxford Street. John had spoiled my day by not being there. How could he have let me down? It was a total disaster. Mum tried her best to bring a smile to my face, but to no avail.

As we forced our way through the crowds, I became aware of a figure charging toward me with increasing speed from the opposite side of the street. This is it I thought, I'm about to be mugged! Suddenly my body was crushed tightly, and a loving kiss was planted on my cheek. I was still very much alive, thank heaven! John's cheery face smiled back at me. He'd overslept, and was so disappointed when he realized, he'd taken a taxi and travelled to London anyway, in the hope of finding Mum and me.

'How on earth did you manage it?' Mum asked. 'There are thousands of people here today, and we could have been literally anywhere.'

'I don't know' he replied. 'I just came up from the underground, and you were the first two people I saw across the road.'

'Do you realize we couldn't have met this easily if we'd planned it?' Mum continued.

My heart was was now bobbing up and down for joy as it danced itself back to life in my chest. 'I can't believe you're really here,' I said, all giggly and starry-eyed. 'It's made my day. I was feeling so miserable.'

He kissed me again. That's what I loved about him, he was so impulsive and full of surprises. Who else would have undertaken such a crazy venture?

A few weeks later I went on holiday. The bingo hall had organized a coach trip to Spain for any customers or members of staff that wished to go. Mum had never been abroad before, and I had only ever been on a school trip to France, so we put our names on the list. John didn't go. I knew it would prove difficult being without him for a whole week, but somehow I would have to manage.

The weather was hot and the scenery tranquil, not the bustling tourist resort that most of us had expected. There were a few good-looking men who worked in the complex, and although I wasn't short on offers of a good time, I missed John like mad and spent most of my time trailing around shops trying to find presents to take back for him. It was a good holiday but I was dying to get back home.

John had missed me too. He hadn't had an easy time of things while I'd been away.

'I'm so glad you're back,' he told me. 'Everyone's been awful.'

'What do you mean?'

'Well' he said nervously, 'one of the bouncers from next door wanted to know what you were like in bed.' Then he went on to tell me about Joan, who worked in the kitchens. 'She said you were a good-time girl, just using me till you got bored. Took my hand and forced it ... said you need never know. They sicken me, all of them. As if I'd touch her. Please don't leave me again,' he said as he took hold of me and squeezed me tightly.

Because we'd been apart for what seemed like an eternity, we decided what we both needed was some time alone together, just the two of us, so we made arrangements for a weekend away.

'Where shall we go, then?' John asked me as we shared a Chinese take-away behind the stage one Saturday after work.

'I don't know. Don't suppose you fancy Liverpool?' I answered.

He tried not to look too despondent. 'I' d rather go somewhere else.'

'What about London? We enjoyed the day trip.'

'Yeah, London sounds good,' he replied enthusiastically.

So we took ourselves off to a hotel in Sussex Gardens, and on arrival we signed in, for the first and only time in our lives, as a married couple. I somehow knew I'd never again see my name written like that. 'So how long have you been married then?' the landlady asked. I can't remember the answer we gave, though I'm sure we contradicted one another. But for this weekend only, John was my husband, and it was wonderful.

By day we travelled on foot and by taxi through the streets of the capital, spending much of our time in and around Soho, browsing around the sex supermarkets for fun, a pair of love-struck teenagers.

I had chosen to wear a black leather mini skirt. It hadn't dawned on me this probably wasn't the best choice of attire for a day in Soho, and I received a few propositions from club owners who tried to lure me into their premises.

After several hours and some lunch we headed back to the hotel by cab. It started out as a normal journey, but turned into something we'd remember the rest of our lives. The usual chart-topping sounds from the radio were interrupted by a song we'd never heard anything quite like. 'Humphrey Davey' sent us into full-blown hysterics; we rolled around the cab in fits. Each time we tried to compose ourselves the chorus would start us off again. Through streaming tears I glared at him, and he glared back at me, but our joyous mood only intensified. My stomach was killing me. The driver thought we were mad. We might have died laughing as we fought to hold on to our sanity, screeching like hyenas, each begging the other to stop. I had never laughed so much in all my life, never been so happy. Our high spirits continued for the rest of the day, thanks to that ridiculous song.

Back in the quiet of the hotel room we wriggled around on the floor trying out the purchases of the day. We really did feel like a married couple; all we lacked was a piece of paper and a couple of rings, and those we didn't need. We had each other. For the first time we could sleep together without fear of having to wake in the early hours and return home. It was wonderful. We snuggled up close; those sea-blue eyes melted into my own, our bodies entwined warm and perspiring, clinging as one. Our spirits homogenized in a heavenly embrace. My limbs trembled with excitement as he lay over me and took the breath from my lungs with a tender kiss.

'I'd like to have your baby,' I whispered.

'I'd like you to,' came a hushed reply, followed by a second kiss. A teardrop spurted from my eye, trickling past his lips and onto the pillow.

'What's wrong?' he whispered.

'I'm just scared. Scared of something terrible happening to you. Sometimes I get this awful sinking feeling. I love you so much and I don't ever want to lose you.'

He brushed my face reassuringly.

'You won't. Don't worry about me, I'll be all right. I'll always be here.'

He held me a little closer. I could feel the gentle thud of his heart on my breast, and I wondered how he perceived mine. My spirit murmured silently unto his. I fell asleep in his arms. Our bodies remained firmly love locked till morning.

Listen to my beating heart soft as summer breeze,
Listen to my beating heart, listen listen please.
Tell me how it flutters, and how it moves in time,
When you lie beside me, perfect love divine.
Tell me how it whispers when you kiss my lips,
And how yours beats in rhythm when I brush your fingertips.
Listen to my beating heart, tell me that you hear,
The love I have inside of me, now that you are near.

We wakened to the sounds of rush-hour traffic and clattering dishes, hot, sticky and without bedclothes. The radiator had been on full, the weather was mild and the room small; we hadn't noticed. It was like an oven.

'This is a joke!' John moaned, as he ran around the room flinging open the windows and grappling with the thermostat. 'At least we don' t have to go down for breakfast, we can just fry an egg on the bed!'

'Let's get married,' I interrupted, 'and spend every day like this.'

'Yeah, I'd like to, that's if I live long enough to get out of this room!' he replied in jest.

'This feels right, you and me like this. Come back to bed,' I whispered.

He leaned over and kissed me. 'Time to get dressed, go out, and show an innocent boy like me around some more sex shops. Never knew such places existed. I have led a sheltered life!'

Back home again we continued to spend many wonderful evenings together after work. Sometimes we would walk, sometimes we would whizz off in a taxi. I never remembered the ride home, only that we had our arms around each other and kissed passionately for the duration of the journey. Once back at my house we would make love, usually on the living room floor. (I had permanent carpet-burns on my back for two years.) Afterwards he'd kneel down at my feet and gaze adoringly into my eyes. 'You're everything to me, everything. I don't deserve you. I don't deserve to be this happy. You're high up there and you're everything. I'm down here and I'm nothing'. He always felt so unworthy of any affection, hard though I tried to convince him otherwise.

'John look at me' I'd say. 'You are everything to me. I love you and you're mine. You will always belong to me, you know that, don't you? Always! Don't put yourself down all the time. You're a wonderful person and you really do deserve to be happy.'

Life was just about as perfect as it could possibly be. One evening, sharing tender kisses beneath the streetlamp outside we held onto each other with all the strength we could find. Suddenly, the world looked flawless. Everything was so vibrant, so strikingly vivid and clear.

'I love you,' he whispered. 'You're so special to me. Everything I ever wanted. I never believed I could feel this way about anyone. You're my best friend, my lover, everything. I'm so happy, so very, very happy.'

'Me too.' We squeezed just a little tighter.

'I never want to let you go,' he continued.

'So don't.'

'Isn't this just perfect?'

'Amazing. I feel so relaxed, so happy so peaceful.'

'It's too good to be true, isn't it?'

'It feels like God is smiling down on us.'

The halo of light from the streetlamp overhead seemed more like that of an angel hovering celestially above us. Our lips eased a little nearer, our eyes became transfixed with a little more intensity and our hearts began to thump just a little more violently at the prospect of stealing a few seconds of pleasure from another world. Then before we knew it, we were there. My feet had no contact with the ground nor my exposed flesh with the bitter wind. My mind was floating, my nostrils intoxicated by the scent of him and my fingers numbed by his silken hair between them. We crushed each other's bodies in a passionate embrace.

No! said the voices inside my head. *Not for this life!* What the hell was going on? Whose voice was this?

'We can't do this, can we?' I mumbled. 'We shouldn't be doing this.'

'I know,' he answered as if he knew exactly what I was talking about.

'What's happening to us?' I gazed up at the stars and thought to myself: This is *it*. This is as good as it gets. Things will never be any better than they are tonight.

And I was right. We were soon to be punished for taking that delicious bite of forbidden fruit.

'You won't ever leave me, will you?' he asked worriedly. 'Please don't ever leave. I wouldn't know what to do if you left me.'

'I'll never find anything better than this. Never be happier than I am right now.'

'Do you really mean that?'

'You know I do. This is what it's all about. This is what love is for me – the moon, the stars and you.'

'I love you so much. So *very* much,' he said, face alight with excitement as he turned and began to walk away from me. He just turned back momentarily to blow me a kiss. I waved him on his way and crept back indoors with a sigh of contentment.

6

The next evening I arrived at work feeling elated and walking on air. John usually arrived about ten minutes after me, so I waited anxiously behind the ticket counter in readiness for him to drift in my direction like a heavenly breeze and bestow a loving kiss on me. But this night was to be different. The cash-desk door opened with force, and my heart quivered as John charged across the foyer, completely oblivious to my existence and impervious to my longing looks. I stood bewildered as he marched straight past me without any acknowledgement of my presence, as though he'd never set eyes on me before. I felt insignificant and rejected. After the usual five to ten minutes that it took for him to switch on the machines I asked what was wrong.

'Nothing,' came a brusque, snappy reply.

Of course there was something; there had to be for someone to change so drastically overnight. Each day after that he' d come up with a different excuse to start an argument. He seemed distant and aloof, wrapped up in a world of his own.

'John, please tell me what I'm supposed to have done wrong. Have I upset you in some way?'

'Just stop hassling me,' he'd reply dismissively.

'I'm not. I just need to know why you're behaving so strangely.'

'I don't want to go out with you any more, OK? You smother me. I never have any time to be myself. Everyone tells me that. You're only my first girlfriend and I'm too young to get married. I want to do things with my life.'

'We can do them together, can't we? I thought that's what you wanted? You're not making any sense. Let's talk about it. Please don't be like this. I love you.'

'Don't say that. You're just confusing me.'

'You said that you loved me.'

'I don't know what I want or what I feel, just Leave me alone!'

'John, *please*!' I'd grabbed hold of his arm in a frantic attempt to stop him from walking away. 'Don't do this to me, I'll miss you.'

'Absence makes the heart grow fonder!' he replied with a sneering grin.

Everything had been so good, I couldn't believe what was happening. One minute it was like this, with me wiping away the tears after agreeing to be 'just friends'; the next it was all back on again. Like a rapidly changing chameleon I had no choice but to adapt to the alteration in circumstance. As a 'friend' he'd offer to walk me home, and I would invite him in for coffee. One moment alone, one kiss, and how could we ever be just friends? All the harsh words were forgotten, albeit temporarily. He'd apologize for his behaviour, say he couldn't imagine a life without me and didn't know why he'd ever suggested it in the first place.

'I'm such an idiot,' he'd say, 'such a fool for thinking I could ever let you go. I hate it when you look at anyone else. I can't believe that you're really mine, it seems too good to be true, and my head gets so mixed up.'

I'd stroke his hair very gently, and let my finger glide over his lips. 'Don't you know by now I'll never want anyone but you? You have to believe that,' I assured him.

'I want to believe you, more than anything.'

'Then believe it. Please believe it. Look deep into my eyes, and tell me I don't love you. That I don't love ONLY you!'

He'd bury his confused head into my lap and I would continue my affectionate stroking. Then he'd gaze up at me with a deeply regarding stare and we'd be overcome by a sense of 'déjà vu'. A slight frown would appear on my brow, the faintest hint of perplexity in his eyes, and the moment took on an air of surrealism.

41

The next day we'd be arguing again over something and nothing. We became quite a talking-point among the staff. 'Are you two on again or off again, then?' Robert would say. 'You're worse than J.R. and Sue Ellen!'

'You can always tell when they've split up,' someone would add, 'they're both dressed to kill!'

It was true. John would wear his black and white outfit, as I liked him in that the most, and douse himself with more aftershave than usual. I'd wear my most revealing black mini-skirt with low-cut white lace blouse, and spend an extra two hours curling my hair and applying my make-up. He'd engage in flirtatious behaviour with anyone and everyone. The more he could see it vexed me, the more he continued, knowing just how I would react, more often than not kicking the money drawers in rage as I emptied them.

'Now now, temper, temper!' he'd remark with a satisfied smirk as he flounced past; a comment that would make my blood boil in my veins and my stomach churn like a fairground waltzer.

I could retaliate by also flirting with other staff members. The tension in the atmosphere was palpable. While I waited in the aisle for the next customer to wave their winning ticket, Andy would creep up behind me and seductively rub his hand down my aching back, whispering lewd suggestions in my ear. John, calling numbers would peer over the top of his glasses when he thought I wasn't looking, his inquisitive eyes watching my every move. I'd tease him all the more, displaying my pleasure; the more envy I could arouse, the more I desired him. We were both playing the same dangerous game, each trying to outdo the other: so you want to make me jealous? I can make you more so!

John's best friend at work was Brian. One night he and I found ourselves alone in the staff kitchen. I was prepared to take things one step further to raise the green-eyed monster, and when for a few seconds our eyes met, a strange urge to share a kiss engulfed us both. I was mainly stimulated by the thought of being seen by either John himself, or anyone else who'd be sure to report back to him on what they'd witnessed.

Even when we were reconciled, he took great pleasure in aggravating me. If I told him I liked his longer hair, he'd arrive next day with it virtually shaved off. If I said I was starting to like the same music that he liked, he'd say that he'd moved on from that, and was now into something different. The more love I showered on him, the more he despised me for it. A strange situation developed for part of his soul craved love, affection and approval above all else. Time and again it was rejected.

I loved to watch him dart around; it was just like watching smoke move. But my stomach would be rigid and tense, waiting and hoping for his eyes to fall upon me, praying for the moment when that icy-cold exterior would break down to reveal the loving, caring person I knew to be hiding inside. Sometimes it would happen. After weeks without conversation, he'd just sail up to me and say something. The words didn't matter, only that I knew he was missing me. The excitement was overpowering, the chemistry amazing. Before the night was over, I'd be back in his arms again. It would always begin with that look: a deep, fulfilling, transitory expedition behind the eyes, for a glimpse of the inner self. Then I would part my impatient thighs, allowing his fingers to explore my saturated body. His lips would brush mine, throwing my senses into disarray. The buttons on his crisp white shirt invited my inquisitive hands to reveal the secret they held; I could not resist. Fully aroused florid lips stroked his warm naked flesh. Falling to my knees, I stimulated him into a frenzy of sexual ecstasy. We would wait no longer. I'd hurl myself onto the floor. He' d follow instantly and lock his sleek, agile frame perfectly between my hips, thrusting deeply inward. Hands clasping mine, together, we reached upwards and outwards, as our bodies tossed and wriggled in a sea of passion, pulsating contractions drawing him further inside, till he permeated my soul. My limbs were paralysed with pleasure, my pelvis oozing honeyed rain, dizziness taking my brain to unforeseen places. Perfect rhythm, perfect timing, perfect love. My cheeks flushed like a summer rose, while my dewy hair clung determinedly to my fever stricken forehead.

'Now I know what they mean by "fucked senseless",' he said with a faint-hearted laugh.

'That was fantastic,' I replied. 'Think I might have a heart attack now. I can't breathe!'

'What a way to go.'

He nestled his head into my breast. A single tear cooled my burning flesh.

'Are you crying?' I asked worriedly.

'I'm just so happy. I love you so much.'

'I love you too. More than you could ever know.'

'I can't believe how lucky I am. What could you possibly see in me?'

'I see . . . everything I've ever wanted. I see happiness every day, forever.'

'You're beautiful.' He whispered.

'YOU too.'

I lay half-dazed, and swamped by a cloud of contentment and calm. My gradually regulating heartbeat quickens momentarily, as my exposed body once again falls prey to his velvet touch. The rain softly taps the window pane, while the bushes scratch and slide against the glass. Shadows dance vigorously in the lustre of lamplight, phantoms of darkness. We are both naked from head to toe, yet warmly clothed in our love. No passing of time can extinguish such a tender moment, a moment when the world belongs to us, and only us. No one can steal it from us. The room had become impregnable. No evil could pervade these walls; there's too much good here. The pain, the hurt and cruel words have been obliterated, leaving only perfection, blissful perfection.

I savoured every second of these intimate moments together, always so short-lived. Sadness loomed close by, waiting to steal our happiness. John could change like the wind. In my arms tonight, it was a pretty picture we'd painted, but tomorrow the canvas might be blank, we might have to start all over again, or it might be damaged beyond repair. We'd never know till the next day. And how could I have known, that beautiful night, that the next day would bring more hostility between us than ever before?

It was Brian's 18th birthday, and Robert had arranged a special surprise. A cake was to be wheeled out just before the interval, and one of the girls was to walk up to him, wearing a long black coat, with only a bikini on underneath. She changed her mind at the last minute, and I was persuaded to take her place. I didn't fancy the idea, as we had a hall packed to capacity. I was shaking with nerves, and given only ten minutes in which to decide. I didn't want to be the one responsible for spoiling Brian's evening, so reluctantly I agreed. It was a decision I would regret bitterly. John was furious.

Sid took the mike and announced that because Brian was now 18, he was entitled to all the privileges that the adult world had to offer, and in I walked swathed in sultry black. I unbuttoned the garment slowly and clumsily, then opened it wide, exposing a great deal of bare flesh, and a two-piece that left very little to the imagination. Whistling and cheering billowed from every direction.

John was enraged. I knew I was in for a hard time of it, once there was a spare moment for him to pull me aside, and I was right. My explanations and apologies fell on deaf ears. I'd paraded myself for all and sundry to ogle at, and he was disgusted with me. I suspect the main objective was a desire for only his eyes to fall upon my nakedness. I found his envy a powerful aphrodisiac.

The tension between us became worse than ever. Every day my laborious attempts at reassuring him became less successful. It became increasingly difficult working together every night, watching as he laughed and joked with everyone else, while I was excluded from the fun. It amused him to belittle me in front of the others. At the end of the night he'd invite everyone except me back to his house to watch videos on his new recorder, and I'd be infuriated. This time he was more determined than ever to continue his avoidance of me. He seemed to take so much pleasure in making me suffer, it was those little things that hurt the most. He would offer crisps to whoever passed by, but not me, apparently revelling in everyone's company but mine.

One night he was on the opposite counter to me, working with Louise. I was in my usual place across the foyer, and could see all too clearly what was going on. For some weeks now, they'd been arriving at work together, his arm affectionately around her shoulders, and much whispering and giggling between them. Tonight they flirted and chuckled incessantly. From time to time Louise's gaze wandered in my direction. I was uneasy and tense, evidently the object of their gossip. I tried hard to smile and carry on as normal, but each word exchanged between them left me more fearful and nervous than the last. Just what was he saying to her? It was all very cosy and intimate. My heart was breaking. How dare he be so happy when I was so miserable? He touched her tenderly upon her shoulder, he was pushing my endurance to the limits.

Anger brewed inside me like a tempestuous storm. The bell rang. Calling was about to commence. He flounced past me with that conceited bounce in his step, and cocked his head into the air, with an expression of complacency. I wasn't worth the time of day.

My blood transformed into molten lava, eruption was imminent. I charged across the cigarette burned carpet, eyes filled with hatred and indignation. Louise was about to bear the full force of my wrath.

'How *dare* you make fun of me!'

She stood small and meek. 'I don't know what you're talking about. I haven't been making fun of you.'

'You bloody liar! You and John have been laughing at me, and talking about me all evening. How dare you! I won't have anyone treat me like a fool, do you understand?'

'But I ... I didn't.' She covered her ever-reddening face, burst into tears and ran off. Stumbling into the office, she proceeded to clock out and collect her belongings before going home.

Shocked faces stared back at me from every corner, staff in bewildered awe, and customers in disconcerting silence. This outburst was totally out of character for me. I always stayed clear of trouble and arguments, though if pushed to the absolute limit as

I was that night, my temper could be quite volatile. Very few people had ever witnessed it, or been on the receiving end. It was my fear Robert would be angry at losing one of his best workers during the busiest part of the evening, but like everyone else, he just seemed to accept it, probably too surprised to say anything. No one dared interrogate me.

I observed John's face throughout the next half hour, as his eyes scoured the hall in search of the absent checker. When the interval came curiosity got the better of him, and he marched up to the cash desk window demanding the answer to the night's most asked question. 'Where's Louise?'

Before anyone else had chance to get a word in, I jumped in. 'I gave her a mouthful and she's gone home in tears. Nobody makes a fool of me.'

His strange expression and deathly silence showed me he was as stunned as everyone else. The tables were turned. Those around me could see I wasn't just a little mouse who could be trodden on. If need be I could fight back, and I would.

Louise and I made it up a short while afterwards. I apologized for my behaviour. I suspected she'd been telling the truth after all, and John had just made it appear as if they were discussing me. He was so good at it, he knew all the moves to make my stomach squirm and my brain rampage. It was so easy to belittle me. People in love are vulnerable and do foolish things, and I never knew what to expect from him. Half the time I was petrified of going into work for fear of what I might succumb to: jealous rages and possessiveness without limit. Or I might be pulled up for talking to the wrong person for too long, or for smiling at some sleazy customer. If I did, he would treat me with all the malevolence that a flirtatious seventeen-year-old deserved. But this time it seemed John had been turned on again by my uncharacteristic behaviour. My actions had made the pendulum swing back in my direction. The ball was in my court. I had him where I wanted him. We were lovers again, and could try to wipe out previous events.

The event of the year was Betty's engagement party. There were about a hundred of us all squashed into her tiny house; I spent the best part of the evening sitting on John's knee. It was the usual party atmosphere: food and drink were crushed into the carpet, furniture flew in all directions, and later everyone grabbed hold of their lover for the smooch of the century. My gaze settled on John, and I realized this was one of those irreplaceable moments. No one else in the room stood prouder than me. No one else's eyes held such fondness and intimacy as ours. No one else's hands touched with such devotion and longing, and no one else's heart melted like mine, when he took me into his arms and kissed me to the sound of those New Romantic hits, as they vibrated the core of our bodies and the earth they stood on.

I wanted him all the time. I needed him all the time, and it was just the same for him. We had to be as close as we could, whenever and wherever the impulse took hold. I wanted everyone to know that John was mine. Our lovemaking created a peaceful unity beyond any stretch of the imagination. When he touched or kissed me it was as if I'd floated into another world, a world of sublime happiness. I'd be completely oblivious to anything going on around me, permanently dazed and dumbstruck. We would hold on to each other so tightly, as if our souls were fusing together, and delve into the eyes, where we could see everything we needed to know about each other. It was exceptional, and we both knew we'd never be able to share this wonderful sense of mystery with anyone else. Our bodies were like an open book. Each wanted the other to learn, explore and to memorize every detail. And we did, night after night.

But perhaps the loveliest times of all were outside in the open, in nature's garden: a hot summer day surrounded by wild flowers and the feeling of what heaven must be like; love, tranquillity and unspoilt beauty. Or walking home on a blustery night, half undressing each other on the way because we were too impatient to wait until we were safely indoors, the darkness enveloping us with its moonlit-tinged cloak. The clock striking midnight in the market place, as my coat blows open violently, and my blouse is undone, the biting wind extending my frozen nipple upwards. My hand grips the steel structure behind – the stall ready for next day's traders to display their bountiful wares. Tonight I display mine. Falling back onto the wooden base I devour the stars with insatiable eyes as they glisten in an infinite sky like a veil of silver confetti, ready to descend on us at any moment. He consumes my breast with hot ravenous lips. My arms cling to his body as the warmth emanating from deep within drowns the icy gale that cuts into my face. I remain safe and warm in his arms.

When you're this much in love, everything seems so much brighter and sharper, more defined than ever before. 'You're only young once,' Mum would say to us.' Make the most of it while you still can; it won't last for ever.' And she was right. When you are young you think you'll always stay that way. You've got your whole lifetime to live. Strange, though; part of me always knew that my whole lifetime was condensed into the brief moments of oneness that John and I shared together. Mum sensed it too.

'Oh no!' she'd say, 'I know it's gone midnight, but I've come home with the safe keys. You two don't fancy taking them back do you?'

'Of course, no problem.'

If the walk back was half as good as the walk home, my feet wouldn't touch the ground anyway, and we'd tread the path a dozen times if the other was there to share the steps. I was as close to paradise as it is humanly possible to be, in a world only meant to be glimpsed through the window of this life. Yet I had done much more than glimpse. I had touched, and felt and lived.

Those voices that were always so clear and concise would tell me: *Look at him! Look at him now and remember how you feel tonight, how happy you are because one day you'll be writing it down. One day you'll have to remember!*

'Who's telling me this?' I'd ask. No answer. What was happening? First the voice told me that John and I were meant to be together, then that our love wasn't for *this life*, and that one day I was going to write about it. At 17, to gaze upon the one person I wanted to spend the rest of my life with and be told, this is the one person I couldn't have, was torment.

I'd stare in bewilderment to the sight of barren trees swaying respectfully to the tune of the wind. Dazzled by heavenly bodies in a vast, sumptuous velvet sky, as they illuminated the deserted streets breathing life into them, I'd think to myself, tonight is a good night. The real John has materialized. But what of tomorrow? Tomorrow I'll arrive at work to see someone that bears no resemblance to the person that lifts my soul from the depths of despair to the realms of glory. I'll be treated with contempt. His face awash with cruelty and harshness, aloof, belligerent and insensitive, he'll reject my advances. I'll become invisible. As he scuttles around, I'll stand helpless, feet rooted to the spot, stomach churning like a turbulent washing machine, feeling angry, hurt, and neglected. Why? What brings about this sudden transformation? How can he tug at my heart and leave me feeling so cold? Why will his eyes seek comfort from every direction but mine? I'll burn with desire, each second becoming more intense. His eyes will brim with hostility as they transmit his thoughts: 'You have no right to come near me!' Mine will convey timidity: 'Who is this stranger before me?' We'll avoid each other like the plague. If only tonight could last for ever, if only tomorrow never came.

Our castle of dreams was beginning to crumble. There were rumours that John had been walking another girl home on my night off – everyone knew except me. I didn't want to believe it, though I had my suspicions. But more compelling than his love for me was the need to arouse my jealousy. More and more new girls were starting work with us, each more attractive than the last, and I began to feel isolated. All the boys talked of which one they fancied most, and I could only wonder if John joined in their conversations. All these eligible young women seemed to be moving in on him, flocking round like bees to a honey pot.

We needed to talk things through properly. I had to know once and for all where I stood, so it was mutually decided we'd meet back at his house after I'd finished work that evening. That night's entertainment were The Merseybeats, and Sandra, an old school-friend of mine, turned up to watch them with me until it was time to meet him.

We had an enjoyable time. A couple of the group members made eyes at us during the performance which boosted our spirits. Sandra cut a pretty figure with her short blonde hair, large eyes and captivating smile, while I caused a stir with my 'long blonde hair and eyes of blue' recalling the lyrics of their most famous song. After a few drinks we picked up enough courage to approach the dressing room and ask for autographs, and once inside they were a little reluctant to let us escape. I was angry with John for messing me around, and I wanted to get even. What better way than to let him know I spent some considerable time locked in the dressing room with a famous 60's band? There was some kissing and one thing led to another, but before the situation got out of control I lost my nerve, made excuses and left, with the promise I'd be back in a couple of minutes. I dashed out of that building as fast as my legs would carry me, chased by feelings of guilt. Guilt over Sandra, who I'd left in there with them on her own waiting for my imminent return, and more importantly guilt over John, who was making preparations to meet me and sort out our problems, while I'd behaved like a frustrated groupie.

I arrived hopeful, though first impressions as I entered his home that night were not good, he said, 'You deserve someone who'll never let you down and break your heart. That person isn't me.'

The tears trickled down my face. He kissed them.

'Please don't cry. I hate to see you cry,' he whispered.

'What else can I do but cry after what you've just told me?'

'I don't want to hurt you.'

'Stop making me so miserable, then.'

He teased my lips into a full-blown kiss. All of a sudden the pain was numbed. I could blot it out for a few seconds, pretend it wasn't really there.

'Put some music on,' I murmured

'What would you like?'

51

'Something old and romantic.'

(The Everly Brothers 'Dream' broke the awkward silence.)

'You know,' he said, 'after everything that's happened, I still need you so much.'

'I need you too,' I whispered with hope in my heart, and eyes still dewy with tears.

'Let's go upstairs,' he suggested.

We hesitated momentarily, and stared at each other. Once again I became lost in the power of his eyes. Ecstasy stirred inside us both: we began to kiss more passionately than ever before. Excitement welled; his heart pounded violently against my heaving breast. Smouldering desire was suddenly unleashed in frenzy. We crashed into the door and shuffling backwards made a frantic attempt to remove each other's clothes before falling onto the bed.

'We just can't stay apart, can we?' I whispered.

'I know. I've tried so hard to hate you, but I just can't find it in me. It just isn't there. I don't think I could ever hate you, no matter what you did.'

'That's because you're not meant to. You know we were *meant* to be together!'

'Yeah, I feel that too. Isn't it strange?'

My heart raced as his kisses took me to the next level of existence. Then, drunk with emotion and with happiness, every breath I took reminded me I was alive; never more alive than that very moment. The tips of his fingers swept lovingly round the curves of my body, and hormones surged through me like river rapids.

'It's cold in here. I'll move the fire closer to the bed,' he whispered, then climbed back in hurriedly, dragging the purple quilt behind him. He disappeared beneath the blankets and imparted tender kisses on my inner thighs, gentle fleeting brushes with warm, hungry lips. We were deliriously happy, and he smelt so fresh and exciting. But there was something else my nostrils had detected, something that marred that deliciously aromatic scent.

'I'm sure I can smell burning' I said, paying little attention to my own words.

'No you can't. Just relax.'

'Yes I can. I'm sure I can.'

'No, no, no, you can't!' He continued kissing enthusiastically.

'Yes, yes, yes I can! John, really I can!'

'All right then,' he replied with a calm look over his shoulder. 'Shit! The bed's on fire!'

The bedspread had slipped down onto the electric fire, and we now found ourselves in a bed of flames. He leapt up quickly and began to smother them but was left with a substantial black hole in his nylon quilt.

'I always knew you were hot stuff.'

'It's not funny, my mum's going to kill me. Look at it! It's ruined.'

I couldn't help but laugh as he ran around the room fully exposed, desperately searching for a suitable hiding place.

As I watched, I wondered why he'd tried to hate me. Why would one person try to hate another if there were no such feelings in the first place?

It was inevitable that we would be drawn to each other time and again like a powerful magnet. We spent so much time trying to make it work. Marrying John was all I could think about. I couldn't visualize a life spent with anyone but him. He had wanted it too in the beginning, so why now did he yearn for a bachelor life? Did he believe that marriage would prevent him from doing all the things he wanted to do? I had no desire to change him. That's why you love someone in the first place isn't it, because of who they are?

We would spend hours sitting on the seesaw in the park, trying to talk it through, or in the nearby blind garden, a restful place filled with the heady scent of orange blossom, perfect for telling him how I was feeling. One such day I remember particularly well. We sat ourselves down on a wooden bench in the golden, mellow sunshine, surrounded by the intoxicating fragrance from the nearby shrubbery. The day was beautiful, but my heart was disconsolate. John had made his sentiments more than clear yet again, and I fought to hold on with all the strength I could muster.

'I love you, John. I'll always love you. I feel I've known you all my life, and I could talk to you about anything. I'll never have that with anyone else.'

'I feel that way about you too.'

'No one will ever love you as much as I do, that's a promise. It just isn't possible for you to be loved any more than you are right now. I can make you happy. I know I can; please let me try.'

'But I don't love *you* any more. You don't want me, all you want is a wedding ring. I've seen another side to you, a side I don't care for much.'

My heart began to drown in a pool of sorrow. 'How can you say that? You mean everything to me. I don't care if I never have a ring on my finger, as long as I have you. Without you nothing else matters. I'll change, if that's what you want. I won't mention it again. Give me one more chance to prove how much I love you.'

'It's too late.' His eyes became fogged with tears. As the first one trickled down his face, I kissed it with such tenderness, the salty liquid fused with my own, and tumbled onto my trembling lips. I moved them slowly upwards, and rested them on his eyelids. Our faces were now moist and dewy. With every new bead of sadness, we clung to each other more, clasping each other in a steadfast embrace.

'Please don't do this,' I sobbed. 'You don't know what you're doing. You don't know what you're saying. You'll change your mind when you've calmed down and had time to think. Don't make me face this life without you, please – I won t survive.'

'You will survive. You'll find someone who'll treat you much better than I can. Treat you the way you deserve to be treated. You deserve so much better than me.'

The tears spurted from my eyes uncontrollably. The pain was insufferable. 'But the past was so good wasn't it? It can be like that again,' I pleaded.

'The past isn't important, it's the future that matters, not the past.'

Great, I thought, a future without me in it? Now, I can see clearly that's not what he meant. He was speaking of our future together, not in this life, just as the voices had told me, but the next.

'I really don't think I'm capable of loving anyone,' he said. 'I don't know what's wrong with me. I keep hurting you, and I'll keep on hurting you because I can't help it.'

'You are capable of loving. You've proved that,' I assured him.

'If it was going to be with anyone then it would be you. If I can't love you then I can't love anyone, ever. I've got to be on my own. I don't know why, I just know I have to live my life alone.'

'Is that what you really want? A life alone, without love, without me?'

'Yes. I don't deserve to be loved.'

'Yes, you do. You won't be happy without me. I know you won't be happy. If you do this, you'll be making the biggest mistake of your life.'

'Well, that's my choice then, isn't it? I'll have to live with it.'

'One day you'll realize exactly what you've lost.'

'I already do!' he replied as the tears continued cascading down his cheeks. 'Oh God!' he cried out, 'What's wrong with me? Why am I throwing away the best thing that ever happened to me?'

'You don't have to. I'm here now, and I love you. Tell me you want me to stay. Please!' We kissed tenderly, our tears merging once again.

'I can't. I have t do this, I don't know why.'

I was confused. Surely love can't be wiped out by a foolish action or inappropriate comment? He was battling against his true desires, trying to convince himself that I didn't matter – *we* didn't matter. There was a great deal of love and desperation somewhere behind that protective mask, but he was keeping it submerged beneath those tear-filled eyes. If I didn't take hold and drag it to the surface it would be lost forever.

Even his friends told him time and again what an idiot he was for letting me go. One evening as they were sitting together in a small group down by the stage with their beers, I glided past in my short skirt and there was a sudden roar of whistling and sexual banter.

'John, you idiot!' they yelled as they slapped him about the head.

'I know I am,' he replied sadly, and his gaze settled on me with an expression of remorse.

Suddenly everyone was on my side, and I was grateful for their support, though it had little impact. The curtain was gradually starting to come down on us.

7

At work, Mum became caught in the crossfire between us.

'Can't you two sort it out?' she'd say.

'He doesn't love me any more,' I'd reply with a defeated heart.

'You just want a ring,' he' d answer back coldly.

'That's not true. You *know* that's not true. Anyway if you really loved me, what would be so wrong in giving me a ring? It's not that big a deal is it?'

'To you it seems to be!'

Mum interrupted. 'But if you really care about John, surely that's more important than any ring? He's what matters. Nothing else should be important. You don't need a ring as proof of his love for you.'

'That's right' John agreed. 'The ring is more important to you than I am.'

'I can't believe you really think that. You two are missing the point here' I said forcefully.

'No' said Mum. 'You're missing the point! What *does* matter more, John or a ring?'

'I can't believe you need to ask,' I said, and with a curt glance in John's direction, 'and I can't believe *you* need to hear it! I thought you loved me enough to want to marry me.'

'Why can't we just stay like we are? Why do we have to keep talking about marriage all the time?'

'I'm not even going to answer that. You don't really know *what* you want, do you?'

'He does love you,' Mum said, with a last-ditch attempt at

getting us back on track. 'Surely that should be enough.'

'It isn't though, is it?' John replied. 'Want, want, want – I'm sick and tired of hearing about wedding rings. I'm too young for all this. I don't need it!'

'Well, bugger off then!' I yelled angrily.

'I can understand how you feel. She's always been the same if she doesn't get her own way,' Mum was keen to point out.

I was stuck fast on the road to nowhere. As I saw it, people get engaged and married all the time, so what was wrong with me wanting those things? If you really love someone, it's the next step you take, surely? I felt like an outcast. Not good enough to be a fiancée or a wife. I would show him. I would show him one day, that there were other people out there who would be glad to have me as their wife. Our marriage would have cemented a beautiful alliance, a partnership made in heaven. The fact that he wanted no part of it irritated and saddened me. We'd been so unified, so in love, so happy, but he wouldn't take that last step, and it broke me in two.

A metamorphosis was taking place, there was another John emerging from within. A John that yearned to be thrilled and stimulated, and above all else, free. My constant complaining bored him, so he began to seek comfort and excitement elsewhere. It became apparent to anyone with half a mind to notice that he was taking an interest in a girl who worked on a jewellery stall in the interval. Her name was Yvonne.

Naturally, I took an instant dislike to her. She had short red hair, a very pale complexion, wore virtually no make-up, and, the most obvious feature as far as I was concerned, she didn't wear glasses. Dressed in the same pair of jeans night after night, (something that John had previously said he hated to see on women, along with red hair), she couldn't have been more different from me. I always put so much time and effort into making the most of myself, but the fact that this girl made no effort whatsoever, and still had John's attentions, unnerved me. He was all over her like a rash. Every interval, he'd be there with his arm around her, making her laugh, and making me mad as hell. Everyone in that place knew John and I were a couple. Making a fool of me was one thing, brandishing the fact before hundreds of people was quite something else.

Whenever I questioned John on the subject, he always denied any romantic involvement, insisting they were just friends, but then one night after work, all my worst fears came true.

I sat next door sharing a drink with some of the girls, when my eyes became rivetted on the table adjacent to ours. There they were, locked in a fervent embrace for all to witness. I thought I was going to be sick. With every warm affectionate kiss bestowed on her, his cold insensitive eyes conveyed a message of destruction directed at me: I'm going to take you apart!

Until then, everything had just been a fantasy concocted in the recesses of my mind. This was *real*. This was proof. He'd lied to me. The one person I'd trusted implicitly, had told me a pack of lies, and the truth was too hard to handle. Sickened and shaky, embarrassed and hurt, I didn't know which way to turn. I stood up and began to stagger in the direction of the exit door.

'Where are you going?' voices were asking.

'I don't feel well. I'm going home'

I stumbled outside and was enveloped in the cold breath of night. Dizziness swamped my confused brain as I clung to the icy metal barrier in front. I sank to my knees, thought I was going to vomit, and started to cough and retch. Tears spurted from my eyes in a torrent of despair. Trembling all over, somehow I found the strength to hold out my arm and flag down a taxi.

One callous incision had severed my life support system. Part of me died that night. I lost faith in myself, and I lost trust in others.

On arriving home, things went from bad to worse.

'Damn you, John! I hope you're satisfied. I hope that you gain some small fragment of sadistic pleasure from violating my soul!' I screamed out loud as I collapsed into a heap on my bedroom floor.

It was the worst night of my life. I cried so much I thought the tears might never stop. 'God, John, do you really *hate* me that much? Why, you bastard, why?'

Head pounding violently, eyes now puffy and swollen. I took some painkillers, then some other tablets that were lying around. They had to make me feel better; I couldn't feel any worse. I sat down in front of my dressing-table mirror, and took a hard look at myself.

'You sad, pathetic, stupid fool,' I sobbed. I could barely see my own reflection through the tears, only enough to realize that the hideous contraption that was magnifying them, had to go. She didn't wear any, so I whipped them off and threw them down in front of me. 'I'll never wear them again. Never!' I shouted. John had always said he liked me in them. Liar! Why had he chosen someone who didn't wear any?

The pain was unbearable. As I glanced over towards the bed, I could picture the happy times we'd spent there, so many of them. I was so tired; tired of crying, tired of pain. My eyes were becoming heavier, and the tears continued mercilessly. My head was getting worse. Wanted to sleep. Wanted to go to sleep and never wake up. My thoughts blurred by suffering. Intolerable pain in my head, intolerable sadness in my heart. I reached for the tablets again. This time they had to work, but no, they gave me no respite. What was I to do? I paced back and forth in torment, working myself up into a greater state of agitation. With one final scream of self-pity and wretchedness, I flopped down onto the bed like a discarded rag doll, sobbing uncontrollably. 'Dear God' I shouted out, 'why is he doing this to me? Why does he take so much pleasure in hurting me, when I love him so much? We were meant to be together, and he's making a fool of me. Why isn't *he* suffering?'

God was listening. I could sense a celestial calmness, and a warm, comforting aura around me, and I suddenly realized I couldn't remember exactly how many tablets I'd taken. My head was so full of pain, my recollection of the last half-hour was blurred. It was probably too many. I called for Mum to tell her what I'd done.

'You've got to tell me how many you've taken,' she said.

'I really don't know. I can't remember.'

'You *must* remember!'

'I can't. A few, I think. Sleeping tablets, and headache pills and those in the blue and white box, and I was drinking alcohol earlier, too.'

I must have blacked out not long after that. The last thing I remember is hearing Mum on the phone calling for an ambulance.

I awoke next morning in hospital. Apparently, I hadn't taken enough to warrant my stomach being pumped, but I'd been kept in overnight for observation. As weak as a kitten, I tried to raise myself from bed, in order to make a necessary trip to the toilet. My legs were like jelly and gave way beneath me. I was so shaky. My heartbeat was feeble and faint. All I could see around me, were very sick elderly people, mostly with heart conditions, and I was overwhelmed with guilt.

One old lady looked at me, only too aware of why I was in there, and said, 'Good lord, girl, you've got nothing to be depressed about. You're young and pretty; you've got your whole life to look forward to.'

But how could I look forward? Impossible to look forward for looking back.

Eventually, after several days' recovery, and no word from John, I returned to work minus my glasses, and with a new hairstyle – a perm that had gone horribly wrong. My contact lens was killing me (I only needed to wear one), and as a result, I could hardly open my eye. A new me on the outside, but still jittery and broken on the inside.

I waited behind the counter for John's arrival. I was shaking with fear. I didn't know how I would react to seeing him for the first time since that dreadful night. I heard the sound of the cash desk door being assertively opened, and I knew he'd entered. Hovering in the background, he looked every bit as nervous as I was. I'll never forget the look he cast in my direction, as if I were the most beautiful person he'd ever seen. Totally mesmerized. I pretended I hadn't noticed.

He was sent over to help, but of course we weren't speaking to one another. I couldn't have found the words to express the disappointment and the anger still reeling round my mind.

As the wave of customers began to flood in, many still unaware of our parting, I was bombarded with compliments.

'You look really pretty without your glasses on. Doesn't she look nice, John?' people kept saying.

'Yeah' he replied. 'She does.'

I smiled to myself inwardly. He was agreeing with them and it felt good.

Yet we still remained silent for four long months, only exchanging words when necessary, during the course of our work. I still fancied him like mad, and still went out of my way to dress up as much as possible.

There was a fashion at that time for long skirts with petticoats and bloomers showing underneath, corset tops and little black cancan style boots. The bloomers felt incredibly sexy. Suzanne had some too. We lay each night on the cash desk floor and pushed hard with our feet on the safe door, when the money bags were overfull, preventing its closure. We flounced around like ladies of the night, our petticoats rustling as we swept up onto the stage. John would cast me that sly look from behind his glasses. I knew I turned him on. He liked femininity. He liked a woman to be a woman, and I liked him to want me, though our airs and graces came crashing down to earth one night when Suzanne bent over too far, and split her bloomers across the backside.

John and some of the others decided to go on holiday to Spain for a couple of weeks. I wasn't asked, and didn't fancy it anyway, just felt a little jealous because John would be spending time away from me, and in another country. I worried that he might succumb to the charms of some drunken bimbo beneath the hot Mediterranean sunshine.

We had our fair share of good weather while he was away, and I spent every day parading around the garden in my pink bikini, listening to the Beatles 'Help' album, which blasted out from the house like a musical hurricane. I tried not to let my imagination run wild regarding John's holiday. Anyway, we hadn't spoken in months. It really shouldn't have bothered me one way or another what he was up to, but I couldn't help wondering.

One particularly hot, sunny day while I was sunbathing, Mum came through from the hall bearing a postcard with a Spanish postmark on it.

Dear Friends,' it began, and went on to tell of hot weather, a good time, and plenty of girls. Jealousy raised its ugly head once again.

'You know, you two haven't spoken in months, then this post-card arrives out of the blue. This means he's still thinking of you,' Mum said. That made sense. If he didn't care, why did he send the card? What was the point of mentioning 'other girls' if it wasn't to make me mad? I began to feel a little better. He was just trying to wind me up, and it had almost worked. He knew me only too well.

I was looking forward to the prospect of him returning home, but all my good spirits were quashed when I accidentally bumped into him, just after he got back. On my way to the town centre to do some shopping one sunny morning, I was stopped dead in my tracks by the sight of a familiar figure advancing toward me. My heart palpitated and my blood pressure soared, as the excitement flooding my veins rose to unforeseen levels. He appeared to be just as pleased to see me as I was to see him, and it was my belief a reunion was imminent. I was wrong.

'Got your card,' I said anxiously.

'Good.'

'Did you have a good time, then?'

'Great, thanks, but you know I almost missed the plane!'

'Really? Why was that?'

'Well,' he replied, laughing, 'I was screwing this girl in a field. You know, in a field!' The look on his face indicated a satisfying event.

It had been me who had first introduced him to the romanticism of making love in outdoor places and I felt this was the ultimate stab in the heart. He even had the audacity to tell me who the girl was – a new girl called Jane who worked with us both, very sweet, innocent and pretty, with blue eyes and blonde hair.

'Right,' I said with a half-hearted grin to disguise my anguish. Twist the knife a bit deeper, why don't you? A tremendous surge of nausea swept over me. Shaking inside with anger, pain and degradation, though I daren't let him see how much it bothered me, I tried to blink away the tears. I wanted the ground to open up and devour me so I could vanish from the face of the earth.

I turned around and began to walk away slowly, legs like lead. His new-found confidence in himself must have materialized from my love. He'd absorbed as much as he could and was now using it like ammunition to destroy me. At least it was just sex, I kept telling myself. There was no evidence of a meaningful, loving relationship, but why was he doing this? Using other people to see what they were like in comparison to me? How could he have stooped so low? The thought of his body interlocked with hers, with anyone's, horrified me to an extent that no words could ever express. The very idea made me want to throw up. My heart was in my mouth once again, my stomach too, and my soul lay crushed somewhere on the pavement I'd left behind me. The walk home was blurred by the images of their lovemaking. I wanted to tear it out, shut it down, eradicate it. I wanted to curl up and die. He was all too aware that he had the power to make my life a heaven or a hell. Maybe that's what turned him on, the power. Having absolute control. With one click of his fingers he knew I'd go running back. The hardest thing to accept was that this just wasn't him; he wasn't really like that, a cruel manipulator of women.

I began to take more and more solace in being with Sandra. She would come over to my house on my evening off work, where we would drink cider and pray to the moon god. The latter only took place when we'd had too much of the former!

I would reminisce on happier times, and pour my heart out about how much I was missing John.

'Sandra, what am I to do? I really love him, and he just doesn't want me any more. In fact he wants everybody but me. How could he have changed so much? Why does he want to hurt me? I'll never love anyone like I love him. I just know I won't. I'm so unhappy.'

'He'll realize his mistakes. That it's you he really loves, and he'll come back.'

I had to hold onto that.

By day, Sandra had a job helping out in a charity book shop. She introduced me to Mark and Clive, who also worked there. Mark had a great personality, always ready to offer support to whoever was in need, no matter how busy. Clive was rugged, A Heathcliff type, with unkempt hair, and a dark, ankle-length coat. He took a shine to me, and the four of us would spend many a day sitting in the back room of the 'Bookplace' drinking tea and coffee, munching biscuits, and talking through our problems.

Sandra organized a party at one of the other nightclubs in the town. We'd been looking forward to it for weeks. Me especially, as I had persuaded John to escort me, but plans for a spectacular evening failed miserably. I had bought a grotesque, unflattering dress which resembled a potato sack with a bit of string tied around it – the latest fashion – so I wasn't feeling my best anyway, and felt decidedly worse when I spotted Yvonne in the crowd.

John left me on my own for the best part of the evening, while he chatted and danced with her. I was left feeling numb. A hall packed with people and I'd never felt so alone. As I downed drink upon drink, a feeling of total worthlessness came over me. Sandra tried her best to bring a smile to my face, but I'd reached my lowest ebb. She stormed up to them both in a blind rage.

'You should be ashamed of yourself. Flaunting your little tart in front of my best friend! Have you got no conscience? Look what you're doing to her! You're a disgrace, and all for this little slag!'

'What's it got to do with you?' he answered angrily. 'Just piss off!'

'It's *my* party, that's what it's got to do with me, and yeah, I will piss off, I'm not staying around here any longer to listen to your crap. I don't know what she sees in you anyway!'

She stared with loathing at Yvonne. 'And as for *you*, you little slag!'

'Don't speak to her like that,' John interrupted.

'Oh, that's right, jump to her defence. Never mind that my friend is breaking her heart over you two. I want you both to leave!'

'Who do you think you are?' John replied. 'You can't tell me what to do.'

'Yes I can, actually, as it's my party. I don't want you here!'

'Well, I'm not going anywhere!'

She pushed him hard as her emotions intensified.

'Don't you touch me!' he shouted.

'I'll touch you if I want to.'

'Sandra, just leave it, please,' I begged.

'No, why should I? I'm not having them treat you like this.'

John wasn't aggressive in actions, only in his bitter choice of words. 'You can't force me to be with someone I don't want to be with. She bores me' he scoffed. 'It's not my fault she won't leave me alone!'

I could no longer conceal my emotions; like bubbling acid they spilled from my eyes. Clive put his arm around me in sympathy.

'You *bastard*!' Sandra shouted.

'I ought to knock you to the ground' Clive added. 'But you're not worth it!'

'And what are you supposed to be? I wasn't aware it was a fancy dress party!' John replied sarcastically.

The bouncers appeared and grabbed Sandra, forcibly throwing her out into the corridor. Clive, Mark and I followed, like three lost sheep in a thunderstorm.

We plonked ourselves down in the lobby, and each took it in turns to find words of comfort for me.

'You're too good for him,' said Clive.

'Clive, fuck off, will you?' Mark butted in.

'Righto, Mark!' And off he went.

Mark had a go at trying to make me feel a little better. Meanwhile Sandra remained livid.

'I can't believe I've been thrown out of my own party, and that bastard is still in there! Weeks and weeks I've spent organizing it and all for nothing. To be thrown out of my own party, can you believe it?'

Clive returned, and I found the strength to smile. 'What's so funny?' he asked with a puzzled expression.

'That Mark told you to fuck off; and you just got up and went.'

'Yeah, well, I've known Mark for a long time now, and when he tells me to fuck off I know he's got a bloody good reason for saying it, and I respect that. I do what he asks.'

Emotions were running high from all directions. Sandra began to argue with the bouncers, as they refused to let her back inside. She was noticeably distressed. 'How can you dare to throw *me* out, and let *him* stay in there? He's the one that should be standing out here, not me! You know me, for goodness sake!'

Clive suggested going back to his place for tea and sympathy, as we all needed to calm down. In a squalling, agitated rampage, we crashed out into the night air.

I took some deep breaths, and tried my best to unwind. I sobbed my heart out, and wondered how much more pain and humiliation I could endure. An invisible, ferocious beast was devouring my heart slowly, and with a contented glaze about its eyes, pulling and tearing, piece by piece.

Clive was attracted to damsels in distress; and I was particularly vulnerable. That night he was there for me, with all the comfort and support I needed. He was my crutch, my walking stick, the only thing I had to stop me collapsing in a heap on the pavement.

One minute I was distressed, then I was angry. I wanted to go back inside and argue; couldn't leave things the way they were. 'He has no right to be with her!' I screamed. 'How dare he?'

Clive pulled me back. 'Come on,' he said, 'let's go!'

Back at his house, we flopped down onto the living room floor with a mug of coffee, and pondered over the evening's events. I remember half a cannabis joint being passed around like a 'peace pipe' and a feeling of incredible sickness. There was a huge picture of Elvis on the wall in front of me, and a plastic budgie on a perch. I began to wonder what the hell I was doing there. Clive, Mark and Sandra were talking, but all I could perceive was a droning mumble.

How could he, after we'd shared such intimacy, such depth of emotion, and unity? I was sitting there in a state of mental turmoil, knowing full well that he'd be inside her before the night was over. I could almost feel the pain of every kiss, the anguish and the torture of every loving touch.

Sandra and Mark were sharing tender moments. Clive wanted me to sleep with him. I sat lost and forlorn, emotionally raped.

'I can't, Clive. I love him too much, you see.'

'It's OK. I understand.'

I ran outside and jumped into the first taxi that rolled past. To my astonishment, Clive jumped in with me. 'Where are we going?' he asked.

'Not sure, I'm still deciding.'

'Fine. That's cool. Still, I'm wondering why I got into the taxi at all!'

'Yeah, so am I. Why did you, Clive?'

'Seemed like a good idea at the time!'

'Think I'll go to John's.'

'That's not a good idea.'

'Probably not, but I'm past caring now anyway.'

On arrival, fuelled with the thought of them up there in his room, and with emotional turbulence beyond all comprehension, I lost control of my reasoning, and took action by throwing a small handful of stones up at his bedroom window. I was so full of anger and bitterness I needed to let some of it escape.

'I don't think this is such a good idea,' said Clive anxiously, grabbing hold of my arm, 'I'll take you home and you'll feel better tomorrow.'

'No I won't! You couldn't possibly understand what I'm going through.'

'Just try to calm down. This isn't the way.'

My tension began to ease somewhat. Clive was right. I was making a fool of myself hankering after someone who wasn't interested. Except that I knew he still was, that he always would be. Just what the hell was he trying to do?

I saw sense and headed for home with the thought that before too long, I'd be able to win him back again.

One day, you'll be writing about this terrible night, said the voice.

'Don't think so,' I replied. 'Don't think I care to remember.'

But you will. One day you'll look back on this night and be able to laugh.

Clive followed me around for weeks, often writing me poetry, and meeting me from work. Though he remained nothing more than a good friend, his presence disturbed John, and that pleased me.

Because of my burning desire to offload my problems onto someone else, I arranged a night out with Geoff, one of the bar staff. He too had lost the great love of his life, so we were both at a loose end. For one night, we could share a few drinks and try to forget; in principle anyway. It turned out trying to forget was low on my list of priorities. Reliving the past seemed a much better idea, and I spent the entire evening talking about John. I found comfort in being able to relate to someone who was in the same position as me, and to laugh again, even if only for a few hours.

'I think the world of him, you know, I don't know what more I can do.'

Geoff must have been moved by my anguished state of mind. 'I'll tell you something for nothing;' he said. 'John cares about you a lot more than he'd like you to think.'

My eyes lit up. 'Do you really think so?' I replied excitedly.

'Yeah, definitely. You know, when I told him who I was taking out tonight, he nearly bit my head off. He was in a right mood, I can tell you. "I don't know what you're getting so worked up for," I told him, "YOU didn't want her!"'

That reassured me. I was still able to rouse envy in him, which was further confirmed next day when I arrived for work. I had just helped myself to a tea from the snack bar, when John stormed up to me.

'Did you do anything with him last night?' he asked, eyes full of insecurity and possessiveness.

I knew what he was referring to. 'No, of course not, why?' I replied.

'Because he's telling everyone that you did.'

I was angry and upset at first, then realized it was probably Geoff's intention to wind John up, rather than shame me. 'We didn't do anything,' I said again.

'That's OK then.' He sighed with relief. 'I knew you'd never do anything like that. Except with me, of course!' He walked away with a satisfied grin, leaving me in no doubt of his unrelenting affection.

Geoff later owned up to the truth when he told John, 'My one big chance, a night out with Amanda. Great, I thought, but she spent the whole bloody night talking about you!'

Deep in the recesses of my mind was still the thought that John had broken my trust by seeing someone else, and on more than one occasion. I decided to follow suit and get myself a proper boyfriend.

I had several penfriends that I'd got to know quite well through *The Beatles Monthly* magazine, and one or two of them had sent photos. The most promising of these was Andrew, so I arranged a meeting.

He seemed quiet, shy and well-mannered. My first impressions were good, but there was one serious drawback I'd failed to notice – he was boring. My memories of our time spent together consist of travelling from his house to mine to the sound of Dire Straits, or spending quiet days in his little attic bedroom having sex.

John and I had been so spiritually close to one another, it had never entered my head I would ever want to engage in a physical partnership with anyone else, and now was no exception. The only thing that pushed me into another's arms and another's bed was the thought of doing unto him what he'd already done to me. I thought we had taken an unspoken vow of chastity, a promise to stay faithful to each other. He'd broken that trust, and now all I could do was follow.

Andrew loved our physical get-togethers; his face would glow with pleasure. Little did he know that I lay cringing, trying hard not to cry, as I opened up my body like a whore. If John could do it, then so could I.

'I love you,' he'd whisper.

'I love you too.' What a blatant lie! There was only one I could utter those words to with genuine depth of emotion, only one to whom those words would ever convey their truest meaning.

Boxing Day, spent at his house, was more than I could stand. I spent half the day crying in the bathroom, and the other half trying not to cry in the living room.

His older sister had recently become engaged, and sat on the opposite side of the room from her fiancé. We all sat up straight. No TV, no music, no conversation, except perhaps to discuss the economic situation in the third world, and above all else, no fun. I could visualize previous Christmases at home – how much excitement John could instil, just by entering a room – and my eyes would fill with tears. Just when I thought things couldn't possibly get any worse, someone suggested playing tiddlywinks. Andrew placed his arm around my shoulder in a cold, stiff embrace, and asked if I was enjoying myself.

'Yeah, great!' I replied with heavy heart, eyes glued to the clock, as I prayed for the day to end quickly, counting down the minutes, until it was time for him to take me back home.

My feelings went no further than pity. He was a nice person, good-looking, and totally besotted with me, which just made things so much worse. His family had little time for him, and in the end that's all that held me back from ending the charade. I wondered how I'd managed to lose myself down a path of existence that comprised no love, no excitement, and no laughter.

I continued with the pretence, and I continued to watch John like a hawk each night that our shifts intermingled. We'd both try our best to avoid any eye-contact. If they were to meet, the situation would become precarious. It was a difficult time. I'd be so knotted and churned up inside, I couldn't focus properly on anything. Working my way through those few hours was like living a nightmare. The only spark of pleasure I could grasp would be at the night's end, when Andrew came to meet me.

I'd slip on my black coat and my black felt hat, with ribbons that trailed enticingly down my back, I'd brush my tresses till the blonde highlights shimmered under the bright neon lights, reapply my silver snakeskin lipstick, and together we'd swan through the main hall. For the first time all evening, John's eyes would fall upon me, and that dose of envy would light up the darkened void between us.

What the hell are you doing with him, when you belong to me? – he didn't have to say anything, the words were loud and clear. You did it to me first. My thoughts swam back across the strained atmosphere.

Then with deciduous rage apparent on a defeated face, he'd turn away from view, and tear past like a ruthless whirlwind.

Within minutes, I'd pick up the latest gossip. 'John's thinking of leaving work,' I heard someone murmur, and my heart arrested for a split second. He couldn't leave me. He couldn't dream of leaving this place. It would be like withdrawing oxygen from a dying person. I'd suffocate without him. He was my oxygen. He was my heart, my soul, my life-force. I would put it to the back of my mind. He was angry, and felt the need to hurt me in any way possible. A spur of the moment announcement that didn't really hold any substance. I would continue my liaison with Andrew, and hope things would soon blow over.

8

Suzanne's 21st birthday party was to be held in the club next door. Andrew and I had invitations, and so did John.

The evening began with tense undertones. I was restless and fidgety. I had difficulty averting my gaze from the entrance door. Who would John turn up with? How would I react if he were with Yvonne again? My last time in there had been an experience I'd rather forget; the last thing I needed was an action replay.

When he did eventually make his entrance, he was with the crowd, Suzanne included, and I found it impossible to concentrate on anything else.

Andrew refrained from dancing, so I sat bored once again, with my head in the clouds, and my thoughts a million miles away.

John tried his best to avoid us. Whenever we did penetrate his field of vision, I made sure the image he saw was of Andrew and me kissing vigorously.

As the hands on the clock pushed away the hours, I decided to dance with some of the girls. It was becoming hot and crowded. Hard as I tried, I just couldn't seem to let myself go. Then 'Enola Gay' by OMD came on, and the music rapidly filled my senses. I spun around in a frenzied whirl, to see that John was also dancing with a small group, and with every pulsating vibration, our bodies began to move closer. Our hearts were beating in unison to the rhythm of the music. Images of reality were blurred by intensity of sound. The flashing lights eliminated all the other faces. The dance floor was packed with people, but all I could see was John. All he could see was me. With eyes completely transfixed, we danced on air. Pure ecstasy. As the music began to fade our hot aching lips grew nearer. My determined eyes fell hopelessly into his. It was not my decision to kiss him, nor his to kiss me, but both, at exactly the same time. Our thoughts perfectly synchronized once again. Our lips finally touched, to the mental image of a thousand fireworks – a mind-blowing, spiritual orgasm of fire! The realization of several hundred pairs of eyes searing into our backs only heightened our pleasure. It was a priceless moment, and those few minutes seemed to last for ever. I never wanted to let him go. We clasped fiercely, squeezing so tightly, we might have died then and there. With the dissolution of our physical senses, came the rebirth of spiritual awakening. The room was ignited with smouldering passion and celestial love. One long, lingering kiss spoke volumes: You're still mine, and you belong to me forever!

Dear God, my heart cried, please freeze this moment for all time. Don't let it end. Please, please don't let it ever end!

But sadly, it did end. When I eventually let go, John walked away with a self-satisfied smirk, knowing full well he could have me any time he wanted, and I was reminded that Andrew had been sitting right beside the dance floor watching it all. I turned to see him disappearing into the toilets in a blind rage. If looks could kill, then I should have been flat out on the floor. As it was, I couldn't have felt more alive, glowing all over, and the adrenalin pumping through my body like a high-speed train.

Rachel stormed up to me and said I deserved a slap in the face for behaving so despicably. That made no impact whatsoever on my smug state of mind; but I knew she was going to tell Mum the following day, and I was bothered about that.

John remained conceited, and flounced around like a cat that had just consumed an extra helping of cream.

When Andrew finally emerged from the gents' room, he sported a red fist and a face like a wet Sunday. He'd been so angry, he'd punched the toilet wall: a better solution than directing his fury at John or at me, he said. Naturally he was upset, and being a nonviolent person, had surprised himself by the intensity of his own emotions.

I'd acted against my better judgement, and I did feel bad, but my guilt was tempered with euphoria. It was as much of a surprise to me as anyone else. I'd temporarily lost control, and thanked heaven for it. I would be forgiven for my indiscretion. Andrew remained so smitten with me, he wished our relationship to continue, despite my recent behaviour.

Mum did find out the next day, and wasn't at all impressed. I couldn't defend my actions, except to say that being with John just felt 'so right'. Being with him always felt right. It was everything else that was wrong.

I stayed with Andrew a while longer, to avoid any more hurt and bad feeling, but as long as John remained on the scene, it was inevitable that more pain would ensue for all involved.

On nights when Andrew was otherwise occupied, John and I slept together. As far as I was concerned, there was no comparison between them. John lit the fires within the depths of my inner self, while Andrew smothered them. I needed John's love like an addict needing a fix. With him I knew happiness and passion. No one else stood a chance.

But there was no escape from the fact that John always desired the unobtainable; once I was conquered, the flame lost its lustre. It would only be a matter of time before someone else's embers glowed more brightly than mine. For the moment heaven's door was open to me. My choice was easy; hurt or not, Andrew would have to go. John was obviously the first to hear of my decision.

'I'll have to finish with him,' I said, as I pressed my lips and my body hard against his, in the comfy paradise of my double bed. 'He does nothing for me. It's you. It's always been you.'

'I know,' he replied. 'I'm such a nice person.'

'I wish you never had to leave. That we could stay just as we are now.'

'Me too, but I will have to go soon. I've got church in the morning.'

'You go to church on a Sunday? Why?'

'Because it pleases my mum. You know she wants me to be a Catholic priest?'

'You're not going to, are you?'

'No way. You must be joking.'

'You should go to church because you want to, not because someone forces you into it. Can't you miss it for once?'

'No. My mum likes me to go. It keeps her happy.'

'If you stay in bed, you'll be keeping *me* happy!' My lips began to make a detailed exploration of his body. All that love inside me exuding through every kiss.

Make it good, said the voice. *Make it as good as you possibly can, so he'll always remember how you made him feel.* I paused for a moment and gazed lovingly into his eyes.

'What?' he asked in swift response.

'I'm going to make you feel *so* good, you'll never want to be anywhere else but here with me.'

I wasn't sure how to break the news to Andrew, and my task was made even more arduous when he arrived next day with an arm full of holiday brochures, ready to discuss the prospect of us going away together.

I dealt him the blow in the only way I knew how, quickly and concisely. He was stunned. He explained that he'd wanted me for his wife.

'I could never marry you,' I told him. 'I don't want to hurt you, really I don't but . . .'

'It's John, isn't it?' he said.

'Yes. I want to be with him.'

'But he'll treat you badly, just like before, you know that.'

'Yes, I do. You're right, but if it only last for a few weeks or a few days, then I have to take that chance. I have to take the opportunity while I still can. I'd like you to try and understand.'

He glared back at me with disbelieving, dewy eyes. 'I really want you to be my wife. I'll overlook this if you promise that you won't see him again. I don't want you to leave me.'

'I'm sorry, Andrew, really I am, but I've made up my mind.' If I had any doubts at all, I had only to remind myself of the tiddly-winks on Boxing Day, and the thought of spending every Boxing Day like that terrified me.

His tears of pain began to merge with tears of frustration. 'You know something?' he said. 'You two really deserve each other!' With that remark he collected his brochures and left.

His mother phoned me some days later, and pleaded with me to give him a second chance, but I had to remain steadfast in my decision. If I didn't break his heart now, I would only break it later.

'He's inconsolable' she said. 'Please, I'm begging you, please.'

'I never meant to hurt him. Tell him I'm sorry.'

Andrew, of course, had been right. After a brief reconciliation which lasted days rather than weeks, it was all over again, just as he'd predicted, and just as I had known all along in my heart.

The two forces were at work once again. One pushing us into each others arms, and the other trying to prise us away. The question was, which would prove the stronger?

After several weeks of despair, rivers of tears, and John's strongest efforts to keep his distance, we were reunited once again, but this time things were to be made even more difficult for us.

Mum became tired of our constant falling out, and the way John had repeatedly used me. She told me he was no longer welcome in our house. Once or twice I defied her, and sneaked him in for coffee. He was always worried about his reception if Mum was still up, and would cross himself before setting foot over the threshold. His face, filled with apprehension, reminded me of an old family friend who used to visit when I was a child. He'd throw his hat in first. If it came back out again, he knew he wasn't welcome, but if it remained on the hall carpet, it was safe to enter.

Whatever reservations Mum might have had, once John was inside she kept them to herself. However, when he was absent, she continued to reiterate her view of him, and there were constant arguments. Eventually I made the decision to leave home.

My sister told me of some girls she knew who lived locally and were looking for a room-mate to share the cost of the rent. It sounded ideal. With my own place, (of a sort), John could visit whenever he wanted. It would be perfect.

In reality it failed to live up to my expectations. The girls were lovely, and so was the flat. We had our own bedrooms, and shared the lounge, kitchen and bathroom. It was fully furnished, spacious and modern, but I found it difficult adjusting to my new life. Getting up in the morning to find an empty fridge or that the bath hadn't been cleaned out properly by whoever had used it last, pushed my patience to the limit, and as we weren't supposed to bring any men back after 10 p.m., there were no more advantages than to living at home.

I moved back to Mum and Dad's after only four days. Mum relented, and John was permitted to visit again. Once more we were back in our favourite room, back on the sofa, and back in each others arms in the place we loved best. After reading some of my poems, he kissed me very slowly and assuredly.

'You wrote these for me?'

'Yes.'

'They're lovely.' For all his faults he could be so sensitive and caring.

'I love you. Maybe the poems will allow you to see just how much.'

'I know you do.'

The bad times would be buried deep. Tonight there had never been anything else but this. My face was caressed with such gentleness, as he made a personal inventory of every detail, no matter how small

All my best memories came flooding back in an instant. Like the time when he, Suzanne and some of the others had gone into town to buy a present for a friend. They'd spotted a necklace in the jewellery shop window with two hearts linked together, one red and one white. As they discussed the possibility of making a purchase, John sneaked in without them noticing and bought it for me. Even though they weren't best pleased with him for stealing their idea, they reminded me how much I meant to him and what a romantic gesture it had been. And there were the memories of sneaking around at work when Mum had told us not to see each other; John leaving before me to make it look as though he'd gone home, then meeting nervously outside the main door, to kiss and cuddle in the shadows, though we could be clearly seen by Mum, and everyone else, on the security cameras that were focussed on the main entrance door. We weren't as clever as we liked to think.

I gazed long and hard into John's piercing blue eyes.

'We're so stupid,' I whispered. 'Why do we hurt each other so much? All we both want is to be together, and we spend all our time trying to stay apart.'

'I know,' he replied. 'It doesn't make sense. I'm sorry for ever hurting you. You really haven't deserved it. I let you go, then as soon as you've gone, I realize how stupid I've been. No one makes me happier than you do.'

'We can't survive without each other.' I kissed him. 'Don't ever leave me!'

'I'll never leave you. Never.' – words that came from the spirit, not the mind. Our minds knew only too well that our physical bodies had to separate for our souls to be reunited. Absence, as we were soon to learn at great cost, really does make the heart grow fonder.

'You know, the stupid thing about all this is, that if we were both dead, we'd be together for ever and ever. Nothing and no one could ever come between us again. They wouldn't be able to split us up. We'd be together always,' I told him with absolute certainty.

'I know, I know,' he replied softly, gazing down upon me, his eyes melting into my own, his arms absorbing warmth from my body as a flower absorbs warmth from the sun. We kissed.

No! Not for this life! said the voices again. I looked at John with dejection.

'It's not going to last is it?' I mumbled. 'We have to try and stay apart, don't we?'

'Yes,' he answered, plunging my heart deeper into despair.

'Being friends doesn't work for us, we've tried so many times. We always need more. There's only one way. It has to be all or nothing, we've always known that.'

Our next embrace carried us both on a tidal wave of passion. 'Make love to me,' I murmured between kisses, 'let me feel you inside.' Once again I found myself bewitched by the velvety touch of his nakedness on my own yearning flesh as he penetrated me. Now, as always, there was a strange warm glow radiating around me and within me. The room was spinning. Those eyes could stop my heart beating as they reflected my love. As I throbbed and moulded myself to the rhythm of his body, we were transported to the dizzy heights of euphoria. My soul lifted itself from the void, as it tried impetuously to reach and blend with his. Suddenly the physical world paled into insignificance.

I was now drifting around the room on a magic carpet of tumultuous emotion, while a million diamonds pierced the atmosphere before me. There were haloes of light all around, like those of angels waiting to guide me on a mystical journey. Little sparks of love rebounded from every wall, as I surged down a river of dreams, exultant, delirious, enraptured. Paradise was within my reach: almost there, higher and higher, closer and closer, my soul waltzed through the heavens. A huge tidal wave approaches; It will envelop me like nothing I've ever known before. Powerful, overwhelming, it crashes into my body with such force, it fills every inch of me with joy and compassion. My soul has been cleansed with love. It exudes from me, warm and sweet. I tingle all over as my spirit returns to its worldly home.

In the aftermath of my exhilarating, but transient journey, I rest in his arms and bathe in unbridled serenity. Tonight we didn't *just* make love. We saw beyond the perimeter, we danced with the angels, we touched the gate of heaven.

'I'd like to put a knife into you now,' I murmured.

'Thanks very much!'

I laughed. 'No, I don't mean it in a nasty way, it's just that if you were dead, you wouldn't be able to leave me ever again. You couldn't hurt me any more. You'd be with me always. We'd stay like this for ever!'

'I know' he whispered softly, 'you're so right. I understand what you mean.'

If we were to have any chance of being together in the next life, now was not our time. We never once questioned this inner knowledge that we both shared. What we were permitted to have now was only a sample of what was to come after.

I sat down on the sofa as I'd done many times before while he knelt, as always, at my feet.

With a deeply regarding stare into my eyes, he uttered those words he'd uttered so often before: 'You're high up there, high up, and you're everything, *everything*! I'm nothing. I'm down here looking up at you and I'm nothing.'

'I'm not everything,' I'd reply in astonishment, 'you are!'

'No,' he'd continue, 'you *really* are!'

I froze. We'd been here before, hadn't we? Suddenly this situation seemed more than familiar. Once again that sense of déjà vu left us both lost for words. We began to see for the first time something more mystifying, beyond the obvious. My God, he was talking of a previous life. Not about him and me as we are *now*, but him and me as we were *then*. We'd lived before!

Still taken aback, I cupped his face in my hands, and words came without thought. 'We've come through many lifetimes to arrive at this point. Our love has survived many things. It will continue surviving. Whatever happens in the future, we'll deal with it, no matter how hard, because we've done it before. Our love is so powerful it cannot be destroyed. Our bodies may be weak, but our spirits are strong, and we'll rise up one day like the immortal phoenix from the ashes. One day everything will come right, I promise. There'll come a time when we'll never be parted again!'

We still had many bridges to cross before then. But now our time was running out fast, I knew I was powerless to stop it.

Before too long I would be spurned and treated with contempt for no apparent reason.

Sure enough, for weeks and weeks subsequently, I ached secretly at his daily flirting, and the humiliation of hearing the girls remark on how much he fancied them. When I helped out in the snack bar he'd often brush past me to collect a drink from the coffee machine before calling. I craved a kind word, a bawdy comment or warm smile, yet he'd remain sullen. I had half a mind to strike him for his arrogance and half a mind to push him against the wall and just kiss him anyway, but I had to learn restraint and play tactfully. Give him a taste of his own medicine. I let him see that I didn't care.

Then one night, I was below stairs in the book room searching for the next batch of bingo tickets. All the serial numbers had to run in sequence, and somehow they'd become all mixed up. I'd been down there for ages when someone must have realized what was keeping me so long. John was sent down to aid me in my search.

Between us we were getting nowhere. I was throwing the books around, he was throwing them around. Our tempers heated, and emotions frayed. I obstructed his path. Or did he obstruct mine? Either way we came to a halt, our eyes screaming desire.

Within seconds we were impaled on each other in a passionate embrace. I wrestled with his shirt, and he with my blouse. With one hand he whipped off his tie and hurled it to the ground, with the other he cupped my breast and sent electrifying shockwaves into my heart. He pushed me assertively against the wall, then disappearing beneath my skirt gently pushed the tip of his tongue into my quivering, moistened body. Adrenalin gushed with explosive force.

'I've missed you so much,' he gasped.

'I've missed you too.'

As we grappled we were knocked off our feet by the messily-stacked ticket parcels, but we barely noticed. The excitement and the thrill of being together again after so long was more than I could stand. His mouth consumed my nipple and once again dizziness submerged my thoughts. Little squeals of ecstasy were coming from my astonished mouth; with increasing vigour. His fingers tenderly formed a seal across my lips. My body was filled with him. I struggled perilously to stay conscious as I began to drift into a world of fantasy. My journey had barely started. One momentary glance upwards and his eyes pierced mine. He focussed on my naked soul. I orgasmed, and began my reluctant descent back to earth.

We tried to compose ourselves as best we could, but when we emerged, all red and flustered, I think everyone got the message.

'It's impossible to find the next batch of books;' John told Robert emphatically. 'We'll just have to start on a completely new set of numbers.'

'You mean you were down there all this time, and still didn't find what you were looking for?' Robert said.

'Well, I wouldn't say that exactly,' John said under his breath.

'What was that?'

'Nothing. The books were in a terrible mess.'

'If they weren't before, they are now!' I added, *sotto voce*.

As our shift came to an end, my elated mood was to change rapidly, as I once again bore the brunt of John's cruelty.

'Shall we go back to your place or mine?' I asked.

'I don't know what you mean.'

'Well, I thought it might be nice, as we're back together again.'

He depressed his card into the clocking machine, and gave me a dismissive glance. 'I never said I wanted to go out with you again.'

My mouth must have fallen open. I don't remember much after that; I was stunned. I felt so ill, so ashamed, so dumbfounded, dirty and used. How could he have abused me like that? How could I face him every night, knowing how he'd humiliated me?

It was impossible for me to continue working there now, under those circumstances. I would have to leave. No doubt about that. I was too ashamed to stay.

9

I left quietly the following week and began work as a hotel receptionist, just a short distance from the bingo hall. The shifts were long and boring. No one was willing to help out if I encountered any problems; I just had to muddle through by myself, often until two o'clock in the morning. My next shift would commence at 7.30 a.m. and I didn't function well on just four hours sleep.

One morning I had an unexpected visitor, a boy called Darren who'd started work at the bingo hall just a few weeks before my departure. He stormed in through the door and thumped his arms down hard on the polished wooden counter.

'I'm really pissed off' he said.

'Why?' I asked.

'Because that bastard has only gone and stolen my girlfriend!'

I knew at once who he was referring to, but I asked 'Who?'

'John, that's who. I'm devastated. You know Jane and I were really close. I cared for her a lot, and then he bloody comes along and steals her from me. I felt that you might understand better than anybody. We all know how he treated you.'

The girl he'd screwed in the field before his Spanish holiday, yes, I remembered her. 'I really loved him Darren. I really, really did, but he used me. He uses everybody then tosses them aside like yesterday's rubbish. He broke my heart over and over again till I couldn't take it any more. That's why I left.'

No one knew better than me how Darren was feeling; I'd been there so many times before. I was still searching my soul to find answers, to make sense of John's actions. What was he looking for that he hadn't already found? I'd removed myself from the building; if only I could remove him from my thoughts as easily.

I continued to meet Mum from work, waiting and watching for him. Will he approach me tonight? Will he speak to me? I spoke to Louise, who was keen to know how long we'd been seeing each other before our final split. She hadn't realized it had been three years. I knew she was enquiring for personal reasons; yet another blow to my already bruised and beaten spirit. The thought crossed my mind, that he'd probably had most of the girls in there. Whatever happened to the sweet, innocent boy I met one late autumn evening in 1980?

After a while, I left my hotel job and began work as a sales assistant in the local department store, only a part-time position, but enjoyable nonetheless. I worked with a good crowd of people, most of whom were blessed with a good sense of humour, and that made all the difference. I got to work in different departments, go on staff outings and training days. All in all, it kept me occupied enough to blot John out of my mind for short periods of time, and life began to look a little brighter. I made new friends, and went on a couple of dates with a boy from 'menswear', who wasn't bad as boyfriends go, but it didn't come to anything.

In my spare time, I made arrangements to meet another of my Beatle penpals, called Robert. We'd spoken many times already on the phone, and his voice was intriguingly Glaswegian. He lived and worked in London as a painter and decorator, and when he told me he could get us some tickets for the opening day of Abbey Road studios, I thought it would be the perfect opportunity to meet.

Our rendezvous took place outside the Virgin Record Store on London's Oxford Street, one hot sunny morning in 1983. As I stood and bathed in the summer sunshine, my thoughts took me back to my last London visit. No trip to the capital would ever be quite the same as that, but nevertheless; it would turn out to be an eventful day.

I was immediately struck by Robert's good looks. He was tall, with a 1974 John Lennon look about him. We sat in Hyde Park, where he sang Beatle songs to me, very well too. Then we bought some ice creams and wandered aimlessly around the HMV store. At long last, it seemed I was taking more control of my life. I could have fun without John, even if only for brief periods, though I still missed him, still yearned for him.

I was 18 years old and couldn't see any further ahead than the present day. The highlight of it, of course was the studio visit. We were interviewed by one of the American TV networks as we queued outside, which was an experience of sorts, and it was fascinating to see all the rooms where the Beatles had recorded some of their most famous hits. There were many lookalikes there that day. Many of them were so convincing, it felt as if I were really sitting next to Paul McCartney, or sharing a cup of tea with George Harrison.

Robert and I got on so well, we decided to see each other on a regular basis. With him living and working in the city, it meant that the only way we could be together was if he came to visit every couple of weeks, and stay at my house for the weekend.

I had to work Saturdays, but the manager was accommodating, and would often let me swap my shifts. On days when I couldn't swap, Robert would wait patiently for me to finish, or he would come into the shop for a chat when we weren't busy.

He was gorgeous. All the women fancied him like mad, and whenever he escorted me down the street, everyone would stop and stare. At night, we would go to a local pub for a basket meal and a cocktail, and afterwards I'd suggest meeting Mum from work, so I could glide towards the bar like a ship in full sail, exuding smugness and serenity.

Both Geoff and John would be serving at that time of night, and while Geoff would be only too ready and willing to accept my order, John remained in the background. One night I caught sight of his arms around the waist of a pretty barmaid, busily preparing some drinks. He smiled seductively, and brushed her ear with his lips. Her features broke into a lurid smile.

I collected my order and whisked it away hurriedly to the nearest vacant table. In an instant, I had been returned to the night John's lips had kissed Yvonne's for the first time in my presence, his eyes conveying lust mingled with sadism, as he contemplated my misery. I trembled nervously, yet excitedly, at the prospect of just one penetrating stare in my direction. For a brief moment his head lifted and his eyes skimmed briskly over mine. His desire was to steal a glimpse. He hoped I hadn't noticed. How could I not?

I took hold of Robert and smooched with him, one eye on Hissing Sid laughing with John at the far side of the bar. Now was my chance to get even – show him what he's missing! Sweet, sweet revenge!

On weekends that Robert didn't come to stay, I still met Mum from work. As I waited for her to finish, it gave me the perfect opportunity to sit with my drink close to the bar, and observe John collecting the empty glasses from the tables. I'd wish and hope and pray that he'd make his approach and illuminate my spirit with a few romantic words.

Sometimes he did. It might just be a brief comment as he charged past, or he might sit down beside me for a few minutes, put his arm around my shoulder as in the old days, and give me a loving smile.

There were the times when, just for a brief moment, every intimate word and thought ever exchanged between us, would flood through our veins and our memories. He still had the power to make my heart flutter like a demented moth around a light bulb, but there were also cruel reminders of his other side.

One night we were chatting in such a way, and my protective shell was just beginning to thaw, when one of the barmaids breezed up to us. 'John, darling,' she whispered, as her arm went around him in an affectionate clinch. Before I heard any more, I stood up and walked off in a childish sulk.

These days seemed far removed from the days when people would refer to John and me as the 'young lovers'. Now it seemed everyone was his lover, or wanted to be. I realized that things could probably never be quite the same between us, so when Robert suggested we become engaged, I jumped at the chance.

We travelled to Scotland to meet his family, and to celebrate our engagement. It was a first visit for me, and it was New Year. What better place to spend Hogmanay? We drifted from house to house, drinking at each one along the way. The hospitality was astounding, but I really showed myself up, and spent most of my time there in various toilets being sick. After everything I'd had to contend with in recent months, I was determined to let my hair down and have a good time. New year, new start. However, spending New Year's Day in bed with a hot water bottle and a stinking hangover, wasn't exactly what I had in mind!

Robert's mum was lovely. She told me that if things didn't work out between us, I would always be welcome in their home. A strange comment to make, I thought, as we'd just become engaged. I began to think that something here didn't seem quite right. Robert shared his flat in London with a male friend. He'd been reluctant to tell him about our engagement, and whenever I'd suggested a visit in the past, he'd always become angry and agitated. I never did see where he lived. He didn't get on well with his father, and I had the distinct impression he was hiding something from me.

On our return home, the engagement was broken off within days. It didn't come as much of a surprise, really. He'd spoken for months about wanting to take me to Scotland to meet his parents, and that when I did, I must have a ring on my finger. It was as if he needed to prove something to them, and once he'd done that I was surplus to requirements. It seemed that all his promises about loving me so much and wanting to look after me forever, had been lost somewhere along the way.

His cousin did phone me from Scotland some weeks later, to tell me that they'd enjoyed my company, and that Robert was regretting his decision. And Robert continued to phone my house from time to time over the following couple of years but we never saw each other again.

10

Mum told me there was to be a fancy dress evening at work, with a competition for the best-dressed member of staff.

Although I was no longer part of the workforce, the manager had said that I would be more than welcome to come.

The next time I met Mum from work, John asked me if I was likely to attend.

'You'll just love the person I'm dressing up as,' he said.

'I might come,' I replied cautiously. 'I'll have to think about it.' I did want to, but I was apprehensive. John might use the opportunity to humiliate me again, and I couldn't face that. I contemplated turning up as 'Boy George', but in the end, after much deliberation, I decided not to.

It was a great night, by all accounts, and John won the competition as, would you believe it, 'Boy George'. He was disappointed by my absence, and asked if he could see me again, so I invited him round for what would turn out to be our penultimate liaison.

We sat beside each other on the sofa, and he stroked my leg. I closed my eyes for a few moments and tried to remember what it used to be like, before all the pain and deceit.

'You know' he said, 'of all the girls, you've still got the nicest legs!'

I suppose I should have been glad of the compliment, but all I could think was that he was making some sort of comparison between them and me. And he went on.

'I've been given many presents by many people, but none of

them were as good as the ones that you gave me. I've been given a right load of junk.'

'That's because I really loved you. I put a lot of effort into buying you nice things because you meant so much to me.'

'I can see that now.'

Whenever we'd been together before I'd always felt so completely at ease in his company, but this time it was different. I was uncomfortable and nervous, more nervous than our very first time together. I'd always been the confident one sexually, John had always been more shy and reserved, at least with me. Now the situation was reversed. I felt as if my every move was being scored from one to ten.

'I've been such a fool,' he said. 'I made a terrible mistake treating you the way I have, but I'll never let you down again.'

No, you won't, I thought quietly to myself, because I'm not going to let you anymore. The love was still there, it always would be, but there was also a sadness I couldn't erase. I knew what had to be done. We made love on the living room floor. For the first time ever it seemed there was something missing. All the magic had gone.

'It doesn't feel the same does it?' I whispered.

'I don't know what you mean.'

'It just doesn't feel the same as it did before. Too much has happened.'

It was the trust, that's what had gone. I had always believed everything he ever told me, but he'd cheated on me so much, I'd lost the ability to understand him or to know if his words were sincere. All the innocence had disappeared. I remembered the naive Catholic boy I had seduced not so very long ago, and how special our love had been, but now it was tainted. In the beginning he was completely mine, but the endless women he'd bedded had put an end to that purity. He'd given part of himself to too many people and it hurt beyond words.

As I held him close every inch of me began to shut down, the life-force draining away from me bit by bit. My heart and my head were filled with remorse as I prepared them for my impending actions. We could never have made it work now. All I could see before me was a future of broken promises and shattered dreams, and the one thing I needed to hear him say was still not forthcoming. I love you. Perhaps if he'd said those three little words it would have made all the difference.

Upon leaving, he took me into his arms and kissed me. 'I'm so happy we're back together again. I really am,' he whispered.

I believe that despite everything those words were uttered with genuine warmth and affection, but I'd finally had enough. My heart couldn't take any more. I gave him one final hug, holding him as close as our bodies would allow, when that mysterious voice delivered its chilling message.

Let him go. If you really, really love someone enough, you can let them go. This will be the hardest thing you'll ever have to do. No good can come of this relationship. He's going to die from the AIDS virus.

My heart sank as my brain tried to make sense of this latest announcement. No it couldn't possibly be!

I released my grip and watched him walk away. On reaching the gate he turned back momentarily, as always, and smiled. He looked so happy and I was so broken. I was allowing him the freedom he'd so craved in the past. The freedom to do whatever he wanted, with whomever he wanted, without restriction, and he was in total ignorance of my plan.

My next step was to go upstairs and write him a letter. In that letter I was to put down all my innermost thoughts and feelings. I told him that I would never stop loving him, no matter what happened in the future, or who I might meet. I couldn't cope with yet another rejection, and it was only a matter of time before we found ourselves in that situation once again. I thanked him for all the good times he'd given me, and explained that I was letting him move on with his life. It was my sincere wish that he find someone who could make him truly happy. Or, if he wanted to play games then he could play them with someone else. It wasn't going to be me.

I couldn't believe what I was doing: letting go of my one chance of happiness with the only person that had ever meant anything to me. I consoled myself with the thought that he was losing more love and affection than he would ever know again, while I on the other hand was losing someone who would have continually broken my heart.

I looked down at the words, but they didn't seem real. I should be telling him in person, but how could I? If I saw him face to face, I might never be able to let him go. I guess it had to be done this way. The letter was sent.

He spoke to me by phone the following day to say he'd received it. He sounded distressed, and asked if he could see me one last time.

'Yes, OK then,' I told him. 'You can come over.'

His face was empty and his heart saddened. 'You won't change your mind?' he asked.

'No. I don't want to do this, but I never really had a choice, did I? We always knew this day would come. I'm going to kiss you now for the last time.'

'Don't say that. That's a horrible thing to say – the *last* time.'

'But it *will* be. I love you too much, you see, and yes, you do make me jealous when you go off with other people. Now I've said it. I can't cope with it any more. It nearly destroyed me once. I can't face that happening again.' He nodded in acceptance. 'I do love you. I always will,' I added. 'That's a promise.'

'You too.' he replied, as he fought to hold back the tears before making his final exit.

As I watched him walk through the garden gate for the very last time, the voices told me I was doing the right thing, but it just felt so unnatural and wrong. My life had ended abruptly. Better if it had, for I wouldn't have been able to feel anything. As it was, I felt an incredible sense of loss. From that moment on, I just had an existence. I'd never again know love or happiness or peace. If I could get over this, then I could get over anything. I suddenly felt envious of all those unsuspecting women out there who would fall prey to his irresistible charms, who would be able to laugh at his jokes and hold him close, while I became just a distant memory. Yet I should be grateful. Everyone knows that the course of true love never runs smooth, and I had experienced something that most people never do in a lifetime. He had been lent to me for a short time, and I should be thankful for that. I could move ahead with all those happy thoughts behind me, at least in theory anyway. In reality it would prove somewhat more difficult.

11

This was the first day of the rest of my life. I walked around in a bewildered daze, despondent and hollow. I'd lost all will to go on. Like a robot, I moved around doing everyday things, but with no soul, no emotion. This abyss inside grew like a cancer, engulfing every part of me. But then, just as I'd lost all hope, I was hauled back by someone who cared enough not to let me drown in a river of my own tears. His name was Robin.

He was witty, good-looking and shared the same sense of loneliness as myself, and the same desire to find someone sincere. He taught me how to laugh again, and introduced me to his friends. John, Maria and I all got on well and we would often venture out at night as a foursome.

They were filled with excitement over their imminent wedding. It would be the highlight of my social calender that year, and I was happy for them, though my joy was always tinged with sadness and envy. They seemed so happy, and to marry the one person you truly love with all your heart must be the greatest feeling on earth. It was the one thing I knew I'd never experience, though I was beginning to see some light at the end of a long tunnel.

John's stag-night was to be held at the nightclub adjacent to the bingo hall, while Maria's party took place at the hotel where I'd worked. Robin and I had invitations to each respectively, and he said that he would try to slip away and meet me later on.

While we were waiting outside in the queue, I told Maria of Robin's plan to meet me later.

'You won't mind if he turns up, will you?' I said.

'No, of course not.'

'If he doesn't turn up it'll be John's fault!'

A disgruntled face turned round from the line of bodies in front of us.

'Thanks very much!'

It was my John. My face turned every shade of red imaginable. 'I didn't mean you,' I stammered, my heart beating so hard inside my chest it was visibly heaving.

Once inside we became separated by the crowd. I danced myself dizzy, not knowing what exactly I was trying to do, so smitten and jubilant at the thought of John in the same room. My reason became lost in a sea of confusion. Who was he with? Was he observing me in secret? I couldn't breathe I was so excited.

At around ten Robin arrived. He was in high spirits; we both were, for different reasons, and I was quite unprepared for what he was about to do. After a few stiff drinks he went down on one knee and asked me to marry him.

I was temporarily elated. 'Yes,' I shouted. 'YES!' I ran to break the good news to Maria, but it was really John that I needed to hear my announcement.

'I'm getting married! I'm getting MARRIED!' I shouted over and over. 'He's asked me to marry him!'

John remained well concealed in the crowd. He *had* to hear it. I had to be sure he'd heard it. There was only one way to be sure, we would have it announced by the DJ. That way everyone would hear. As the words came over the mike people everywhere began to cheer and clap, and my stomach did unlimited somersaults. The song that followed was 'Baby Love' by the Supremes, and I glided across the floor singing at the top of my voice like Tweety Pie on roller skates.

Amidst the felicitations I noticed John slip quietly away. Was he upset? Or had he finally had enough of my singing? In those few seconds I suddenly sobered up and began to function like a normal person once again. It was as though someone had waved a magic wand of stupidity over me then taken it away. John's exit had broken my period of enchantment. Cinderella had gone to the ball and danced her heart out all night to the sight of her Prince. Now midnight had struck, the Prince had vanished and she was returned to her pitiful self, a sad, pathetic little nobody, who'd once had it all then lost it. As his shadow left the building, that invisible cord that bound us so fiercely together tugged a little harder at my heart.

I couldn't help thinking how special it would have been if John had asked me the same question, and the celebration had been ours.

Robin meant a great deal to me, and I knew this was my way forward, my chance of a new life. It would also be my ultimate revenge on John. We'd revelled in flirting with others, he'd broken my trust and my spirit in describing his sordid little escapades, now I would go one better. This act would cause maximum destruction, and I wanted to do that. Wanted to make him feel the same intensity of pain I'd suffered at his behest, This was my trump card and I would play it.

Planning the wedding gave me something to look forward to, and that was something that had eluded me in a long time. I heard rumours that John had booked a holiday abroad, so he'd be as far away as possible on the day itself. If that was true, then it was obviously affecting him as much as I hoped it would. Had it been the other way around, I would be feeling totally devastated, and utterly unable to cope.

When the day arrived, my little guardian angel popped up again. *If you make these vows today, you must never break them!* That I knew instinctively already. Because of my faith in God, I could never retract those binding promises, however much I might want to. You make a commitment before God, in his house, and it's sacred, otherwise there's no point. The voices had continually told me that the happiness John and I shared wasn't for this life, so what else could I do? It was beyond my control. I didn't want to live alone for the rest of my days. I had to try and make the best of it. With Robin I thought that might be possible.

Maria was my bridesmaid that day, and we shared a few

sherries in the kitchen before leaving. I'd been looking forward with trepidation for weeks, and now the moment had actually arrived, it was a bit of an anti-climax.

As is traditional, I followed everyone else, together with my dad in the wedding car, a 1950s black and cream Phantom V. Sitting in the back and feeling like royalty, I became a little girl again. I remembered how I would dress up in Mum's old net curtains and parade around the streets. It had always been my dream, from as far back as I could recall to wear a gorgeous white dress, and sweep up the aisle to the man I loved, waiting for me at the altar. And here I was, sitting in the white dress, but the man of my dreams was far away. God only knew what he was thinking.

In a few hour's time the life I had known before would be all tidily in my past. It was 30th March 1985. A day of sunshine, showers and blustery winds. I don't remember much about the walk down the aisle, as I suspect the sherries had taken effect by then, and I was in awe of all the people, mostly work acquaintances from the bingo hall, who seemed to be staring straight through me, as if they could read my thoughts.

When it came to the part where the vicar asks if anyone knows of any reason why 'these two people may not be joined in matrimony', I had a vision of John charging through the church like Dustin Hoffman in *The Graduate* to whisk me away, but he didn't.

We couldn't afford to go on honeymoon straight away, so after the reception, which finished at around teatime, we went home, got changed, and went back out again for an evening meal.

By the end of the day I was shattered to say the least. So much had happened in such a short space of time, it felt like a dream. The day was over before we knew it. It was as if it had never really happened, only in my mind. But it had happened. I was someone else's wife, and I wasn't sure I'd done the right thing. I did love Robin, but it was a different kind of love. Whenever he touched me, I'd withdraw like a shrinking violet. *You're betraying John by being with anyone else*, the voices kept telling me, and I knew I was. I felt John was my husband, and I was being unfaithful to him by being with Robin.

However, Robin *was* my husband according to the law of the land, and I had to try and get a grip. John was part of my past now. I'd done what I'd done, and one way or another, I had to live with it. Maybe in time things would change. My views might change. Come on, Amanda, I told myself time and again, you've got to learn to let go. There's no going back now, it's too late.

Being married wasn't going to be as easy as I'd first thought. Sharing your life with someone else takes some getting used to, and we had our fair share of arguments in those early years, but we learned to compromise. Eventually, we learned to like the same things. It was all about adapting to someone else's needs.

When my wedding photo fell off the wall in the living room rather suspiciously, I wondered if it was an omen. Did it mean that our union was wrong? I had reached a point of no return, now; I discovered I was going to have a baby. That gave me something else to look forward to.

I heard on the grapevine that John had recently left the bingo hall to work as a nightwatchman in a nearby factory, and following a short, unsuccessful period of time as deputy manageress in a well known ladies' fashion store, I returned to work there myself, oddly enough this time as *his* replacement. Being back in that place was heartbreaking. I had so many happy memories from before, and it was hard not to see John walking down the aisle, selling tickets, or serving behind the bar. We'd shared so much love and so much laughter. I'd been so full of dreams, dreams that our lives would always be filled with love and laughter, and now here I was, back there alone and pregnant with someone else's child. There was a sadness I couldn't eradicate or put into words. I pictured him wherever I looked. It was as if part of him would always be in that building, and yet I felt only half a person without him physically there.

When it came time for me to leave, I knew I'd pass through

those doors for the very last time. I wouldn't return. I couldn't bear to open them again to all those memories.

My little girl was born a couple of months later, and it now seemed I had everything I had ever dreamed of. Why then did it feel as if there was still something missing?

Thoughts of John were perpetually trapped in the labyrinth of my mind, and I wondered how long it would be before a day might pass without him filling my head.

My daughter was lovely, and I decided to throw myself into bringing her up. It would clear my mind of other things.

Then one night Mum offered to babysit, so Robin and I could have some time on our own. We went to a fairly prominent town bar that had been recently refurbished, and while we were waiting to be served, I noticed a crowd of men nearby in boisterous spirits. 'Happy birthday, John!' one of them shouted.

I turned around immediately, with the hope that it just might be, and it was. He was standing right there beside me, looking in the opposite direction.

'Yeah, Happy birthday John!' I joined in.

He spun around quickly at the sound of my voice. 'And you!' he replied. He'd so readily remembered that my birthday followed his by only three days.

We were both a little flustered, and lost for words. I couldn't think what to say next, so I introduced Robin. Although they acknowledged each other, the atmosphere was distinctly frosty. I had told Robin of my relationship with John, and I think he realized it had been special. He turned away, in an effort to reach the front of the drinks queue, and was unaware of what happened next.

'How's your daughter?' John asked.

'She's fine,' I replied excitedly. 'Totally mad!'

He turned his back on me swiftly, and took comfort from the drink he'd left on the bar. I knew he was hurting, and trying hard to conceal the pain. After several seconds' pause for composure, he turned back and looked as fondly into my eyes as he ever did. His hand swept over my poker-straight locks with loving tenderness, and my heart was ignited once again. Like the sun's golden rays, his warmth penetrated my open soul. I was once more captured in that web of magic and mystery.

'Your hair,' he said. 'It's still the same!' His eyes were as bewitched as the very first time they ever feasted on me.

I'd been growing it long for some time now. I knew he preferred it that way.

'Yeah, it's still the same,' I replied, 'still long.'

Our eyes were screaming out to each other. His were screaming *Why*? and mine were screaming *Sorry*. We wanted to say so much, and could utter so little. The words just wouldn't surface.

Within moments, Robin returned to whisk me away. He was somewhat annoyed, and said that John and I had been flirting with one another. He was quite right, we had. Thankfully, he hadn't seen John touch me in such a loving way.

I felt a warm, happy glow inside me. It was apparent he still loved and missed me, as much as I did him.

Whenever I made a trip to the ladies' room or the bar, our eyes would meet again, and all our sadness, emptiness, regret and pain would amalgamate. We could feel each other's heartache, and each other's longing.

As time passed by, and that night was left reluctantly in the far corner of my mind, I lived in hope of seeing him once more. I tried hard to get on with my life. Some days were easier than others. Sometimes I longed to pick up the phone and dial his number, just to hear the sound of his voice and ease my troubled mind, but I always resisted the temptation.

After a while, I heard he'd moved somewhere near Gatwick, so the chances of us meeting again became even more remote.

Robin and I got on pretty well most of the time, but I missed John's friendship, and his love. He understood me as no one else ever could. He knew my own feelings before I did myself.

12

It had been a particularly bad year. I had been married for three years, and on the weekend of my anniversary, which was also Easter that year, I suffered a miscarriage. I had just begun to recover from that, when Robin's father died on my daughter's second birthday.

To raise my spirits, God had a surprise in store for me. One sunny day after Mum and I had taken a walk through the woods with my daughter in her pushchair, we decided to call in at the town centre bakery and treat ourselves to some cakes.

'Hello,' said a mysterious voice from behind. Recognition wasn't instant, but my heart skipped a beat at the sound of that warm, familiar tone. It was John, and I couldn't believe my eyes or my good luck.

I recall I was wearing a revolting peach nobbly jumper that I thought was lovely at the time, and my denim skirt, but I did have my favourite earrings on, my make-up was decent, and it was a good hair day, so I hoped and prayed I resembled the teenage Amanda of his memories. I had retained my slender figure, which I was quite proud of, and I stood tingling with apprehension.

'Do you think she's changed?' Mum asked.

'No, not at all,' he replied. 'She still looks just the same as I remember.' I breathed a huge inward sigh of relief.

'God, it must be about four years since I last saw you!' he added.

It was actually only two, as the last time had been just after the birth of my daughter, but I knew what he meant. It had certainly felt more like four years.

'How's married life then?' he asked.

'Yeah, it's good. We have our arguments and I storm off, but I always come creeping back.' What the hell did I say that for? I was so delighted and taken aback, I didn't really know what to say about anything.

'What are you doing with yourself these days then?'

'As little as possible, just a housewife, you know. So not much really.'

'Dossing around then, same as ever,' he said with a smile.

'That's not fair. I worked really hard when we were together at the bingo hall.'

'Yeah, I know you did.'

'What about you?' I asked cautiously. 'Are you married yet, then?'

'No.' I breathed another inward sigh of relief. 'I was living and working near Gatwick, and there was a girl down there. If it was going to happen it would have been with her, but it didn't. I'm living back here now.'

Mum left us alone. I think she sensed that we needed some time to ourselves, but neither of us could find the words to say what we really felt, and anyway we didn't need to. It was all in the eyes: that desperate need to kiss once again. And I wanted to kiss him, wanted to put my arms around him and tell him that my feelings hadn't changed. He wanted it too, but we held back. We had to. We could only stare with despairing adoration.

'Until the next four years then!' he said with defeated heart, as he began to walk away. As I watched him disappear from sight, all the things I really wanted to say came flooding into my head. I had the strangest urge to run after him. I might never see him again – that's what crossed my mind. What if this was to be the very last time? Do something! Run after him before it's too late! I just can't let him go like that. All these irrational feelings, where were they coming from? Why should I be thinking like this? I'm only 23, he's only 24, preposterous to think that I'll never set eyes on him again. I was in a panic, the like of which I had never known before. *It's all right*, said the voices, *you'll see him again before you die. God will allow that. Before you die, you will see him again!* I began to calm down instantly. I accepted what was said to me. I had no reason to disbelieve what I was being told, and I could live with it. Of course God would let me see him again if I played by the rules, I just knew it had to be true. With the assurance of seeing him one last time before leaving this life, I felt reasonably contented.

The years began to move slowly onwards, albeit with lead in their boots, and I moved out of town to a large village nearby. I had another baby girl, and spent my days doing housework and gardening while listening to music from my past, bringing back happy yet distant memories. Day after day the unmistakable sound of ABBA's 'One of Us' screamed heartfelt messages through my open window, as if their poignant words could fly across fields and towns on a breeze and deliver my wistful thoughts to his doorstep. And the waiting persisted, and my soul lost the ability to feel or to care.

Robin was a good husband, providing a good home and plenty of money. He never gave me cause to be jealous. It took something like ten years for me to stop thinking of John at least once a day, and even then there were still times when his loving words and sarcastic humour absorbed every available spare inch of brain capacity that I had. When Robin and I quarrelled, I would fantasize about turning up at John's flat in my black coat, with nothing underneath but my naked body to tantalize him. I understood him to be living in a town flat some 20 miles away, not that far, really, from where I lived. But I had a family to think about; I had made my bed.

Memory is a wonderful thing. I must have spent hours and hours just remembering. I could close my eyes and see John playing football on the field opposite his old house with me sitting in the corner watching, or the look on his face when I presented him with the scarf I'd knitted in West Ham colours. Or us making love in a cold enamel bath with hot steam and water splashing onto the floor, damp lips on my silky-soft breast, bubble-bath foaming, and wet tongues wrestling, while outside streetlamps burnish the sparkling midnight frost in a winter landscape.

The time we'd argued, and the next morning I turned up at his house to find him still in bed, removed all my clothes, crept in beside him and kissed every inch of his sweet tender body.

'I'll give you something to confess when you go to church tomorrow, and you going to be a priest as well!'

'I know. It's absolutely disgusting it really is, and me such an innocent boy! What do I know about sex? Oh yes, now I remember!'

I loved the way he would speak to me sometimes, and roll his eyes heavenwards as if to say, 'Where did *that* come from?' There were the memories of sadder times too, like the night I went down on my knees in the middle of the town centre, and begged him not to leave me. How much I'd cried, and how hard I'd tried to hold on to him. That stony-hearted look, that preceded the words, 'I don't want you any more! Just Leave me will you?' He prised my fingers from their tight grip on his clothing. 'Please John, please!' I screamed. Part of me wanted to close the door on those images so I couldn't be hurt any more, and part of me wanted to remember every tiny detail, every day of my life.

Every time I heard the word 'AIDS' on the television, or in a newspaper, my heart would sink. The voices in my head that had told me so clearly how John's life would end, and yet it was hard for me to take seriously.

The months and the years continued to drift by. Another spring, another summer, another autumn, another winter. I developed new interests, and made new acquaintances.

Whenever I went out, I always made sure I was well-groomed, just in case John and I met unexpectedly. Had he ever married or had children I wondered? Did he ever regret losing me? On days when I was deep in thought about him, was he also thinking of me? There was so much I wanted to know about his life, and so much I wanted to tell him about mine. It would have been lovely to meet and reminisce about old times over a coffee. I had managed to move on with my life, but I'd never managed to let go. It had never been possible to let go.

I moved house again. Still remaining in the same village, only this time our conservatory business had paid for what most people would describe as a dream home. A large barn conversion with a courtyard garden, and views of the valley from several rooms.

Over the years we enjoyed filling it with period furniture and inexpensive antiques, and I suppose that's how I filled my days, by making a nice home for my family, and trying to forget. I was safe in my own little world. So lucky, everyone was thinking, to have all that before the age of thirty. Small compensation for what I really wanted.

I became very friendly with the American lady who lived next door. We went shopping together, and enrolled on a flower-arranging course. She would often appear with trays of freshly-baked muffins or banana bread when Robin and I were out in the garden, or invite us in for a glass of champagne. They even bought presents for the children at Christmas, telling them that Santa had visited their house first. She and her husband appeared to be genuine, caring people. Everyone was taken in by them, probably no one more than me. I was still so gullible I believed anything that anyone ever told me.

One day, they suddenly announced they'd be gone by the end of the week, and disappeared, leaving a trail of debt behind them. They had promised to keep in touch, not only with us, but with others in the village they'd latched on to. No one ever heard from them again, and it saddened me that human beings could be so cold-hearted to one another. Very few people seemed to be genuine, I found, and I discovered I would be better off without anyone except my family. Robin felt much the same. Sometimes it seemed as if we were the only two people in the world who didn't get off on using and hurting others.

Over the years I took comfort in eating and drinking large quantities of red wine. I put on two stone in weight, and although I went through an aerobics phase for a while in a bid to get myself toned up, I had succumbed to being a couch potato.

What would John think of me now? Gone were the days when I had a shapely figure, and my lovely legs that he once so admired were now riddled with cellulite, varicose veins and stretch marks. The shape was still there somewhere, and luckily I could still manage to conceal the less delightful aspects of my body with appropriate clothes and shoes. Everyone still told me I looked good, but then they never saw me without my clothes on. My long blonde hair that he loved so much had now been transformed into a chin length, graduated bob, and was no longer in spectacular condition. All in all, time had taken its toll on me, but then as Robin continually reminded me, I was a woman with two children, not a teenager any more. He thought I looked better than I ever did.

The new, less adventurous me, filled my days with organizing children's parties, attending school plays, cooking, cleaning, and going on family holidays. The very little romance that had existed between Robin and me had, over time, dwindled away to nothing. We were good friends, and that is all I really wanted from him. He was someone to share my life with, and in that respect, he fitted the bill ideally.

We celebrated the millennium in Gran Canaria, and as we put the 20th century firmly in the past, I wondered what the future held for John and for me as we led our separate lives. What did this new era have to offer?

I was 35 years old now. The television screens were filled with artists from the 'New Romantic period', Boy George, Spandau Ballet, Visage, the list was endless, taking me back to a place in my life where I wished I could stay for ever. It seemed such a long time away now. I was another person then. Young and alive and full of hope. I wasn't sure if that girl still existed any more.

My stroll down memory lane returned me to the three phases of our love. The time when John was in love with me, and I couldn't reciprocate; the time when I became enamoured of him, and he was no longer smitten with me, and the wonderful time in between, all too brief; when we both shared love together. Divine bliss: when his love and mine both reached the highest level of attainment at the same time, and we belonged only to each other, entirely, completely, totally.

I had plenty of time to reflect, while I lay by the hotel swimming pool on New Year's Day 2000 with my glass of wine as the January sun's comforting rays beamed down onto my pining heart.

Throughout that year John was in my thoughts constantly, I believed because it was the first year of a new millennium, and reminiscing was high on everyone's agenda. It would turn out there was to be a far more significant reason for my failure to let go of my past, but it would be a while yet before I was to realize exactly what that reason was.

13

I kept thinking about organizing a bingo-hall-staff reunion party. It would have given me the perfect chance to see John again, and a good excuse to contact him by phone, but I thought long and hard about where it all might end. How would we feel if we saw each other again? Would the same feelings still be there after so long? Perhaps he'd been able to let go of his past. Perhaps I should leave things well alone. The idea niggled away at me all year. The only way we were ever going to see each other again was if I arranged it, and it had to be soon. If I was going to do anything, it had to be done now.

By the end of the summer I had still organized nothing. Part of me still believed that if it were to happen it would be by chance, God's decision, rather than mine. I couldn't interfere with fate.

It had always remained the greatest mystery to me, why John had treated me with such animosity when he loved me so much; a question I'd asked myself a thousand times. Why had he tried so hard to hate me? Then one day, completely out of nowhere as I was busily getting on with the housework, it just came to me.

It was because you weren't Catholic. That's what it was all about. It was all over religion, said the voice.

I switched off the vacuum cleaner and stood motionless for several minutes. It made so much sense. Why hadn't it come to me before in all those years? The message was so clear and left no room for doubt any more. I could suddenly see why he had left my house in such a foul temper. Why he'd tried to hate me and distance himself from me and his true feelings by forming relationships with other girls, each time without success. Why he would finish with me, then walk off in tears. Not the actions of someone who wants to rid themselves of somebody. How stupid could I have been? He could hide behind that ruthless exterior, that was the easy way, to make me despise him. Disguise his true character behind a framework of severity and harshness. He could do it so well, and would have almost been convincing if it weren't for his eyes. The hard-hearted, cold-blooded creature had eyes filled with love, that he could not disguise.

Mum and I discussed John at length over the coming months. It all started when I was compelled to buy two videos, *The Thorn Birds* and *Jesus Of Nazareth*. For me the story of *The Thorn Birds* had a poignant meaning. I could, just as in *Wuthering Heights* identify with the characters, each longing to be with the other, battling against feelings that could not be denied.

Jesus of Nazareth I found fascinating. It made me think about the more important issues in life. Over and over I kept watching both films as if I were under instruction from some invisible driving force.

I began to think more than ever before about the relationship that John had with his mother. It seemed he'd been continually torn between his love for me, and his duty to her. I would have happily changed religion for him anyway, but something told me it still wouldn't have been enough. Perhaps if she'd known how much I really loved him, it would have.

The younger brother whom John had paid to leave us alone all those years ago died some time in the mid-90s. I could still see the two of them arguing in my mind's eye. His father also passed away that decade. He must have been devastated. My thoughts had been with him and once again I had considered making contact, but my life was so far removed from his by then. What would I have said? He would have probably needed love and support that I was in no position to offer, so I reluctantly abstained. His world was slowly falling apart, and I was powerless to stop it.

Then in the autumn of 2000, life began to take a very strange turn. Mum hadn't been feeling well and decided to take a much-needed visit to the doctor. As she sat in the surgery waiting room, she became aware of a man sitting directly opposite. She didn't immediately recognize this person in his late 30s with slightly greying hair and glasses, but he was keen to scrutinize her.

She began to feel somewhat uncomfortable as the eye-contact from the dark-haired stranger across the room intensified. Why would a man half her age be staring so profoundly? Maybe she had a hole in her tights, or maybe her slip was showing beneath her skirt? All these irrational thoughts were flooding through her mind. Does this person know me?

It wasn't until the doctor called her name and she proceeded into the examination room that she finally realized who it was.

'I saw John in the doctor's surgery today,' she told me when I telephoned later that day to ask how she'd got on. 'I'm sure it was him. It *was* him, only slightly older.'

This was good news. If he was still in the area, I was still in with a chance of bumping into him. If it could happen to Mum there was no reason why it shouldn't happen to me.

Later that afternoon, Mum received a strange phone call. Whoever it was just listened, then hung up. We thought this a strange coincidence to have happened on the same day that Mum had observed John in the medical centre. She'd kept the same phone number all these years, and was still listed in the directory.

A fortnight after, she saw him again. They passed each other briefly in the town centre, and this time he spoke.

'All right then?' he asked.

'Yes, fine, thank you,' Mum replied, as she kept on walking.

In retrospect she was angry at herself for not entering into more conversation with him. But that's life, isn't it? You always seem to realize what you should have said or done after the event. When informed of this latest encounter, I somehow felt sure he'd been to the chemist to collect his repeat prescription. I didn't know why the thought suddenly crossed my mind, or why my yearning to see him again was becoming more profound than ever before. There was a compelling need to phone him and ask if he was OK. But why wouldn't he be? Except that John wasn't the kind of person to visit a doctor without good cause.

I had been taking my daughter regularly to the local diagnostic centre for the past few months, and one afternoon while we were waiting, my eyes became rivetted on a teenage schoolboy sitting opposite. It was crazy, but this boy looked exactly like the John of my memories. He was wearing a near-identical school uniform and suddenly I was cast back 20 years. I tried hard to avert my gaze. Then within minutes a thought broke unexpectedly into my reflections: why hadn't I seen John come in here for his blood tests? I was taken aback – I couldn't possibly know if he'd been in for blood tests. It didn't make any sense. But I just knew that he had. I knew without knowing how I knew.

Over the following weeks, more and more strange sensations would pass through my mind and my body. I might be calm and relaxed, happily watching television, when I'd suddenly be overwhelmed by a tremendous pressure inside my head. Not a headache, there would be no pain, just a combined feeling of panic, anxiety and desperation. It would reach its peak within minutes and last for about half an hour. I felt as if my head were going to explode. It seemed I had no control over what was happening inside. I'd try to relax with deep breaths or a glass of wine and eventually these emotions would subside. They would just come from nowhere and fade to nothing.

Once Christmas had passed by and we entered the New Year, my thoughts of John reached unprecedented frequency. Every-where I went I hoped and prayed we would meet. I looked for him around every street corner, and decided to purchase a mobile phone, something that had previously held no interest for me. A ridiculous thought, as he wouldn't have had my number anyway; but I kept thinking, I've got to make it easier for him to get in touch. I've got to see him soon. Time's running out. Why, after so long, was he suddenly in my head 24 hours a day?

I wasn't the only one feeling like this. Mum also started to think and speak about John more than she had done in years. We spent virtually all our time reliving past times.

'If you could have just one wish now, what would it be?' she asked.

'To see John come through that gate, like he used to,' I replied with sadness, as I glanced towards the front garden.

'You'd like that more than anything?'

'Yes, more than anything. He gave me the happiest days of my life.'

'Why don't you give him a ring?'

'And say what?'

'Hello.'

'Yeah, right, after all this time! Anyway I'm married, aren't I? No good can ever come of it.'

'It wouldn't do any harm, as a friend.'

'No. That's the one thing that we could never be. If we spoke, then we'd want to see each other. If I saw him again, that would be the end of my marriage. I couldn't give him up a second time.

'Perhaps you're right.'

I knew deep down that God would be the one to bring us together when the time was right. I just had to be patient.

In February I caught pneumonia. I was very ill for a number of weeks and it seemed as if I might never get out of bed. My heartbeat was weak, I couldn't breathe, and I felt totally drained. Even the slightest movement became a cumbersome chore. The antibiotics took a long time to kick in, but once they did, I began my slow but determined recovery.

During my period of convalescence I was awakened with a start one evening by an uncomfortable presence at the foot of the bed. It was the same uncomfortable presence I used to sense when I was little, just prior to my out-of-body experiences. There was nothing visible with the naked eye, though it was obvious I was being observed. It was just as if a portion of the darkness was alive and breathing. I began to suffocate. My heart rate became erratic as I fought to take in some air. I leapt up and ran into the bathroom, lungs gasping, body tingling and consciousness fading fast. This sinister force seemed to be draining my oxygen away, and I struggled perilously to hold on to the minuscule amount that I had left. With a splash of cold water onto my face I took hold of the sink as the room began to rotate. Slowly but surely, my breathing steadied. The presence vanished, and I began to feel better. I was left shaken and frightened.

A couple of weeks after, I was to encounter an equally disturbing episode which came in the form of a dream; an unusual dream, not like any I'd ever had before. When I woke up next morning, I could recall it vividly. I was standing in front of John's mother and she was dressed in black. John sat to our left, also shrouded in darkness. I could only see half of him, a sort of side view. He was watching and listening intently. I took his mother's hands into my own, and told her how I'd always loved her son with all my heart. John remained silent, but deep in thought. I kept wondering why I couldn't see the full image of him and why no words were exchanged between us. Why don't we speak to one another, I kept thinking, and why can I only see half of him?

The images I saw that night haunted me throughout the week. As with most dreams, I had no idea what it meant, but it played over and over in my thoughts, along with an overwhelming need to see John, which was undiminished. Over the next fortnight these feelings would reach a devastating climax. The same message would infiltrate my mind insistently each day. *Time's running out! Time's running out!*

Why was time running out? I was only 36. I'd never experienced this kind of panic before in my life, so why now?

On Monday, 2nd April 2001, I headed for town on a mission. My goal was to find John one way or another, and I bordered on the hysterical as I scanned every face in the crowd, hoping that his might be one of them. My agitation was indescribable. John, where are you? Where *are you*? my thoughts were screaming. I've

114

got to see him today, it must be today! With tears welling in my eyes, I tried hard to transfer my thoughts to him. If I concentrated enough, then perhaps he might just get the message: 'I *need* to see you, John, and it *must* be today! I searched and searched till I sent myself dizzy, though my efforts were unsuccessful. He just wasn't there.

With my feet dragging and head hung low, I bumped into Jeeves. A series of strange sensations passed over me. I'd been thinking so hard of John, and the one person we'd shared a rapport with had suddenly appeared before me. He offered me a crisp, and at that moment my heart seemed to accept reality. There was no point in searching any further. My pursuit had proved fruitless. A sinking feeling enveloped me and I decided to go home.

Tuesday was pretty much an ordinary day, except that on waking, I felt lethargic and listless, as if a heavy weight had been placed over my chest. I could still breathe, but it was arduous and laboured.

On both Wednesday and Thursday I remained agitated, but it was on Friday that my thoughts of John reached fever pitch. By Friday evening I was so full of panic I didn't know what to do with myself. I felt restless beyond all comprehension. Pull yourself together, Amanda, I kept on saying, these feelings are totally irrational and unfounded. Calm down, for goodness sake! My head was filled with desperation so profound I had difficulty controlling my emotions. Someone else seemed to have absolute control of my mind.

I needed to phone him. If I heard his voice and knew he was OK then I'd feel better. I wanted to do it there and then but it just wasn't possible. The family were at home. There was no privacy anywhere. I'd have to wait as best I could till the next day, when I knew they'd be all safely out of the way at a football match. All I had to do was make it through the night.

Saturday came and I woke feeling nervous and perturbed. I knew what had to be done, yet I was going against my better judgement. I

115

had always prided myself on being honest and open about everything, now I was about to behave very uncharacteristically.

After everyone had left for the match, I copied John's number from the directory, climbed into the car and drove to the supermarket as fast as I could. I couldn't phone from home, as Robin always made a point of scanning the itemized bill in detail, and as we lived in a bad reception area my mobile would have proved useless. This was the nearest place from which I could ring him.

As I sat in the car park shaking with fear, heart pounding like mad, I began to dial the numbers. There was an unusual noise, followed by a message. 'There is a connection fault. There is a connection fault.' I knew I had the right number. What was going on? I kept redialling but each time the words were the same.

'Where are you, John?' I shouted. 'Where the hell are you?' Something was very wrong, I could sense it.

I scuttled around the store picking up items of food and thoughtlessly throwing them into the trolley. There was only one thing on my mind that morning and it wasn't the weekend shopping. Where was he? Why couldn't I get through?

Afterwards, I went on to Mum's, believing a cup of tea and a chat might help me unwind and loosen up a bit. I decided not to tell her about the events of the previous 24 hours. How could I explain what I didn't understand myself? It was Grand National day, and as usual we had a small bet on, though the main topic of conversation that afternoon was John.

'I wonder what ever became of him,' Mum said.

'I'm surprised he never died from AIDS,' I replied coldheartedly. I don't know why I said that, it was a horrible thing to say. My mind was still in a state of mental anguish and confusion, and Mum could sense my agitation.

'You're in a strange mood today' she said. 'What's wrong with you? You're in a world of your own.'

'Am I? I don't know. I just feel really keyed up and anxious. Not too sure why.'

On the way home I called into the local petrol station to fill up. While I was waiting to pay a voice came into my head and told me to buy an evening newspaper. There was a large pile of them sitting on the counter in front of me.

Buy the paper!

I argued with the silent voice. 'I never buy a paper on a Saturday. There's nothing in it.'

Buy one!

'No, I really don't want one.'

Buy it! Look in the death column!

No, I said to myself, John wouldn't be dead, and if he's got married then I don't think I want to know anyway. Right up until the very last minute, I wrestled with my conscience over what to do. Before I knew it I was being served, and there was a long queue forming behind me. Will I? Won't I? Will I? Won't I? I was about to pick one up, then hesitated. No, I won't bother. I paid for the petrol and left.

I stepped from the car to the sound of a ringing phone. It was Mum and she sounded distressed.

'Amanda, what was John's middle name?'

My mind went completely blank for a few seconds, but I knew what was coming next. 'I can't think. I can't.' Then it came back to me suddenly.

'Amanda, I don't know how to tell you this but ... John's dead!'

I was struck dumb. I wanted to say something but the words wouldn't come out.

'Are you still there?'

'Yes,' I muttered. 'Still here.'

She began to read the obituary announcement. He had died on Tuesday 3rd April, from a short illness. All my worst fears had come true.

'Oh Amanda, I can't believe this. I really can't. We were just talking about him.'

'I know,' I replied. 'We were, weren't we?'

'Are you all right? You don't sound surprised.'

'That's because I'm not, really.'

After all, the voices had been preparing me for this moment for almost 20 years. Sometimes I'd even been asked how I would react if I were to suddenly learn of John's death, and now it was upon me.

'It won't sink in for some time you know. Won't hit you properly yet.'

'I'll have a drink,' I answered. It was all I could think of.

'Don't do anything silly, will you?' she asked worriedly, knowing just how great an impact this news would have on me.

'No, I won't.'

I placed the receiver down, and fell to my knees on the living room floor. The tears flowed incessantly.

'No, John, no! What have you done? Why did you have to go and die? Why did you have to leave me?'

It didn't seem real somehow, couldn't be true. There must be a mistake. Someone else with the same name perhaps. Even though the age and family names Mum read out to me were correct, it just couldn't be him. But for all the doubts in my head, my heart knew the truth. This was no mistake.

I tried to compose myself before the family returned home. It wouldn't look too favourable if I let Robin see how upset I was over this. I knew I'd have to attend the funeral, there was no doubt about that, so I would have to tell him of John's death. But when I did, instead of sympathy, I received a barrage of abuse. First he hurled various insults about John at me, then questioned my reasons for wanting to attend the funeral. It was the last thing I needed after the day I'd had. All these years he never knew of my true feelings, and I felt his response was unwarranted. John *was dead*. What did he feel threatened by? I needed support, but he made it clear I would receive none from him.

Nothing on earth would prevent my attendance at that funeral. John had been a godsend to me. He deserved my respect, and my presence at his final departure. I hadn't been there at the end of his life when he needed me, but I could do this for him, and I sensed that he wanted me to. I knew I'd have to approach his mother, just as I'd done in my dream. I had to tell her of my undying love for her son. He needed to hear me say it, and he needed her to hear it.

14

The funeral was set for the following Wednesday, and I knew there was much to do before then. Mum had also expressed a wish to attend, and it was comforting to me to know I could count on her support. I was aware from the newspaper announcement that his body was to be brought to the chapel of rest for a few days. I desperately wanted to see him. I needed to see for myself that he was dead, or else I might never believe it to be true.

On the day of his reception there I made a spontaneous decision – as I was driving past, I had a sudden urge to stop the car. Anxiously I dashed inside.

'Is he here?' I asked nervously, and gave his name.

'Not yet,' I was told. 'Later this afternoon.'

'Would it be possible for me to see him?'

'Yes, I don't think that will be a problem, but we'll have to check with the family first.' I left my name and number.

Later that day they told me that my request had been refused, apologised and said it was out of their hands. Without the family's permission there was nothing they could do for me.

I wanted to be close to him, wanted to see him one last time. It had been so long, but would I have been able to cope with seeing him like that? Perhaps it was better to remember him as he was. I could only respect their decision.

A couple of days later we ordered the flowers. Engulfed by emotions beyond my control, I felt something was telling me they had to be white, so I decided on lilies. I deliberated long and hard over the message that would accompany them. What on earth could I put? What could I say that would be appropriate, without drawing uneccessary attention to myself? After several discarded scribblings I decided on a couple of lines inspired by *The Thorn Birds*, ending with the words, the best is yet to come.

Meticulously I planned my outfit, making sure I had the correct black attire. John always favoured me in black. He hadn't seen me in a long time and I knew he'd be watching. I needed to look my very best. I had been brought up to believe that when you attend a funeral you should dress impeccably as a mark of respect. As the day of the funeral drew nearer, the atmosphere at home became more strained. I worried how I would cope with the event itself, and was apprehensive of approaching John's mother after all this time. Then, too, I had to keep my true feelings as deeply within me as I could, so as not to alert my family to the extent of my anguish. How would I hold it all together? My emotions were in a turmoil the like of which I had never known.

The obituary announcement had mentioned a partner, Karen. Though I was curious about her, she didn't really matter too much to me for as far as I was concerned, my presence in church would be far more significant than hers. John's funeral couldn't possibly take place without me.

My shoes were polished, my clothes were pressed ready and waiting. The day had arrived. I drove to Mum's, and together we set off.

'This is it, then,' I said.

'Yes. If someone had told me when we all worked together, and I watched him night after night selling tickets, that he would be dead at 37, and I would still be here at nearly 69, I would never have believed it. I'm nearly double his age. It seems so unfair.'

'It still hasn't sunk in. I still can't believe it's really happened, and this day is here. I keep thinking I'm going to wake up from this, but I'm not, am I?'

'No,' she replied softly, 'you're not.'

As we pulled up outside the church, I noticed many people milling around, and many faces that I didn't recognize. It felt weird. Everyone was probably wondering who I was; I was wondering who they were. Without knowing it, I had parked my car next to Suzanne's. We chatted briefly in the car park where she told me that Brian and David (another of John's close friends,) had the grim task of carrying the coffin.

I took a deep breath and began my sombre walk through the heavy oak church doors. Once more I was overwhelmed by an internal voice, but for the first time in my life, I knew whose voice it was.

She's here! She's here!

I seemed to be picking up John's thoughts. When he was alive, I could almost read them. Now he was dead it was as if the barrier had been lifted. The coffin was placed ahead of us in the centre of the church. A photograph had been placed on top. I wasn't close enough to see the picture in detail, but could make out that he was dressed casually, slightly heavier than I'd remembered and still looking gorgeous. It felt most strange to be suddenly staring at that familiar face that I hadn't seen in so long, and in such macabre circumstances.

We sat by the aisle about halfway back and directly in line with the coffin. I found it hard to accept that everything I had ever lived for was lying in that box before me. Part of me was dead, part of me was still here and part existing in a world I didn't fully understand. Suddenly I felt three dimensional. Droves of people began to pour in, followed by the family. Most of them looked just the same, only older. A small plump woman with long dark wavy hair, whom I took to be Karen, sat down at the front and waited attentively for the service to begin. The church was now so packed with people there was no more sitting room left. I observed a scattering of single women, many of whom appeared understandably upset, but the majority were men, no doubt friends from football clubs, and work associates.

The most poignant speech came from David. He told us of the four most important things in John's life – love, friendship, music and football – and of a person who hated to let anyone down, that even when dying, he had still got up from his bed to go into work. A person who would suggest a trip to the seaside at two o'clock in the morning, and had once boasted of going without sleep for four days. Many of us would recall being on the receiving end of his cruel sense of humour, but would also recognise that he was a very lonely person, who had at the end of his life found happiness again with Karen. To the many former partners assembled, 'John would have wanted me to say that he loved each and every one of you.' He had perfectly summed up the John of my memories, who after 19 years hadn't really changed a bit. He was describing the person I'd fallen in love with.

As the service drew to a close, it was announced that the family had chosen a song to be played. I couldn't hear the words properly, and I didn't know who the vocalist was, but the song was recent, that much I did know. I assumed it related to his time spent with Karen. It must have been their song. It was called 'This Year's Love'.

The coffin was lifted high into the air, as John embarked upon his final journey. It passed over my shoulder, and as it did, the most incredible wave of sadness and regret passed over me too. I wanted to touch it or kiss it, or stop it for a few seconds to say my own last farewell, but I couldn't. No one could see how my heart was breaking. Everyone else could mourn openly. I had to mourn in private, to keep it all inside. I was married to someone else. I cried, as did the others, but I daren't let the true depth of my heartache show.

Sitting next to Mum was someone else in a considerably distressed state. She was familiar to me, and to Mum.

'Who is that girl?' Mum asked.

'It's Yvonne, isn't it? The one he left me for.'

'You're right,' she replied, 'it is.'

She was the one with the pasty face whom John and I had quarrelled over such a long time ago. It seemed insignificant now. We were united in our grief.

I could feel John's presence all around. I knew he could see me, at least I could sense that he was watching, and was pleased I'd been there.

As everyone made their way outside one of the ministers began to stare at me, as if he were hypnotized, then walked past everyone else and came straight to me.

'One of the chief mourners has left some gloves. Would you see they are returned to them please?'

'Of course,' I replied politely, as I took them from his hands. I smiled inwardly to myself: 'chief mourner'! No one was mourning more than me.

'That's it,' said Mum. 'That gives you the excuse to speak to his mother. Of all the people here and Brian said that he counted about three hundred, he walked up to *you*, as if he was in some sort of a trance.'

'He did, didn't he? I thought I was imagining it, but he did seem to select me in particular.'

'What do you make of that song they played?'

'I'm not sure, but you know, music is going to be the link.'

'What do you mean?'

'Just that. Music will be the link between us.'

Mum looked puzzled, and I felt puzzled. I wasn't really sure why I made that comment, but I did. Perhaps I was in some kind of hypnotic trance too.

'That comment about John going to the seaside at two o'clock in the morning and going without sleep for four days – those are the actions of a restless mind. Someone who can't find happiness,' Mum said.

'I know. He searched everywhere but could never find it. I was the only person who could fulfil that need in him.'

By the time we emerged from the cold, dark building into the tepid spring sunlight, most of the cars were already on their way behind the hearse. We were among some of the last to arrive at the cemetery, yet secured a place directly at the foot of the grave.

The gloomy chill of Easter wind whistled aimlessly around the graveyard. Daffodils on nearby burial plots bobbed incessantly behind black silhouettes. To the sound of 'I am the resurrection and the life', the coffin was carefully lowered. I'd never been as close at any funeral. My heart ached with a sadness beyond words, though I knew he wasn't really down there but somewhere close by, watching. Many people threw red roses down onto the coffin; I observed pensively as Karen threw hers in and cried out how much she was missing him. I had nothing to throw in except my undying love and a small handful of earth I'd managed to grab from a container someone was passing round. As I dropped it onto the wooden box the name plaque glistened in the sunshine. Behind that shining piece of metal was the face I'd cried a thousand tears over, the face I'd taken so lovingly in my hands and kissed so many times. Eighteen years previously, for the very last time, and it seemed like only yesterday. I looked up briefly. That rose-tinted glow on the world now seemed tainted by opacity. He made the sun shine brighter, the birds sing sweeter, and the moon dance in a velvet sky. With his exit went that lustre that painted the world such a pretty place, leaving it grim and cold.

The first thoughts that entered my head as I gazed down into that hollow ground, were 'may you not rest, as long as I am living!' God, what a terrible thing for me to think. The words came from *Wuthering Heights*, and though I had no idea why they came into my head I wholeheartedly believed in their truth: he would not be able to rest in peace while I remained on this earth. 'Wait for me!' was the next thought I had. 'Wait for me!'

After everyone had finished saying their goodbyes I turned round to see Karen walking away from John's mother. I knew my moment had arrived. With determined steps I marched forward. 'I must speak to you' I said forcefully. She looked somewhat puzzled. I embraced her, then took her hands into mine, just as I'd done in my dream.

'I loved your son with all my heart, truly I did. There hasn't been a day in all these years when I haven't thought about him. Wondered where he was, or what he was doing.'

'Thank you for that,' she said, smiling.

I glanced briefly to my left; and nodded slightly, as if to let John know I'd done what he wanted of me. I knew that as in my dream, he was there, watching and listening. Suzanne asked if we could be expected at the local community centre, to share a drink in celebration of John's life. I didn't feel much like drinking or celebrating, but I said we'd go. As we entered the hall, people seemed to be staring at us from all directions, but Brian, Suzanne, David and John's mother were all sitting together at the far end, so we joined them.

David stood up, and gave me a warm embrace. 'Amanda, it's so lovely to see you again after all this time.'

He knows, whispered a silent voice inside my head. I took the voice to be John's, and that David knew John's true feelings for me.

I sat down, and listened intently as they spoke of the missing years. I heard that he'd had a motorbike accident about five or six years previously, and hadn't been in very good health since.

'What did he die from?' I asked Suzanne.

'Well, he actually died from pneumonia, although the family are saying it was stomach cancer. No one really knows for sure.' But I did. I didn't need anyone to tell me, I just wanted confirmation for my own peace of mind.

'He had a lot of bad luck in the last few years. He suffered a lot, you know, after losing his brother. They said it was a short illness, but it wasn't. He hadn't been well for a long time.'

I suddenly remembered the night I'd taken the tablets, and my question to God, 'Why wasn't *he* suffering?' Now it seemed I had my answer.

He'd been admitted to hospital about two weeks previously, when I had the dream. Brian had been sent for at the last possible minute, though the family had advised him not to enter the intensive care unit.

Suzanne explained that his last job was in a food factory just a stone's throw away from my village, in fact pretty much in line with my house. Considering he lived over 20 miles away, Mum and I found this quite amazing. 'Talk about wanting to be close to someone!' Mum said. 'Of all the factories in all the towns, he ends up just a couple of fields away from your house.'

It did seem strange. More than strange.

I asked John's mother, 'What terrible illness could have taken him at such a young age?'

The look on her face was enough; anguish and humiliation. 'Please, I don't want to talk about it. I really *don't* want to.

That was all the confirmation I needed. I was aware that AIDS sufferers often succumb to pneumonia at the very end, often following multiple tumours, many of which are internal and can affect the digestive tract. For want of a better phrase it is often described as a 'short illness'. The small pieces of information I'd secured, together with the family's reluctance to discuss any aspect of his illness, led me to one conclusion: the voices that I'd heard 18 years ago on the day John left my house for the penultimate time appeared to have been correct.

It suddenly came to me that the most important people in John's life were all sitting together. Karen remained firmly at the opposite end of the hall. I wasn't sure if she knew who I was, but in any case we did not approach each other. I toyed with the idea of introducing myself and offering my condolences, but thought better of it. After a brief chat about old times with the select few at our table, I hugged John's mother one last time before leaving.

When we got back to Mum's, I was overwhelmed by the sense of peace that seemed to fill me. Like a brightly glowing candle internal warmth filtered through my veins, with such calmness and tranquillity it was almost celestial. The last time I'd experienced anything on that scale had been twenty years before. There was a huge sense of relief also that I'd made it through the day without falling to pieces or making a fool of myself. I believe I'd acted with dignity.

Mum read the obituary again and concluded that John hadn't died peacefully. 'You know,' she said, 'the family haven't put peacefully in their announcement; it is usual. Strange, for such a religious family.'

That seemed to be coming through to me too. At the point of death his mind and his soul were troubled, as mine would have been if the situation had been reversed.

Some days later there was a further announcement in the paper thanking everyone for attending the funeral, and for the floral tributes received. Karen had put her own message in, describing wonderful memories during a *year* spent together.

15

Mum said that John's death would be a release for me in a way, enabling me to get on with my life. She couldn't have been more wrong. I had made the decision not to return to the cemetery again, not wanting to offend or upset anyone. I'd done what I had to do, and that was that. I was to be proved wrong too.

My mind was tormented with guilt. I should have made a visit to the hospital before it was too late. God only knows I had enough warnings. I was the one who should have been there to help him, to offer comfort and support, to hold his hand. Why hadn't he sent for me? How could he? He had no way of contacting me, except through Mum. He had tried to make contact by power of mind. How could I have been so stupid not to recognize the signs? All those panicky feelings, all those times I felt my head was about to explode, the agitation, the fear, I now knew why but it was too late. I had had my chance and missed it. I felt dreadful. Whatever we still needed to say to each other had been left unsaid. How frightened must he have been? Powerless to halt this destructive illness from devouring his body, he would have suffered in silence, telling no one, not even the closest members of his family, until there was no other option; and I knew. I knew all along, all those years before. I might have been able to prevent it, told him to take more care. All that time I said nothing, just waited. Waited for the news I hoped would never come. How would I ever be able to forgive myself? I could picture the scene: his body ravaged by disease and pain, his lungs gasping for that last breath of air, and spirit screaming out in vain for me to pacify his troubled mind.

Over the next few days depression began to set in, made more burdensome by the fact there was no one with whom I could share my sense of loss except Mum; so I found myself spending all my available spare time with her. She seemed to understand my suffering. Strangely enough she was feeling almost as bad as I was. 'You know, Amanda,' she said, 'I feel terrible, absolutely terrible. As if I'd lost my own son! It doesn't make sense. I can understand why you feel the way that you do, but why me? I've been on this earth for nearly seventy years, and I've never experienced anything like this before. I thought the world of my mother, and I was devastated when she died, but I feel more loss for John. More than I did for my own mother! What on earth is going on?'

One day soon after, Mum was taking a walk near home, pondering over recent events and thinking how sad it was that John should be lying in the town cemetery at just 37 years of age, when a bird suddenly landed in front of her. A strange silent voice penetrated those thoughts. *But I'm all right. I'm all right*, said the voice, leaving her paralysed with bewilderment for several seconds. It was to be the first of many strange events. Over the following weeks things were to become a great deal more eerie for both of us.

Strange sensations began to take control of my body. The shivery feeling that people describe as someone walking over their grave, would happen to me four or five times in succession, all the time, every day, over and over. A tremendous surge of energy would be transmitted through me. Beginning low down at first, then working its way upwards, again and again and again. The nearest description I could give would be to say that I felt like a radio trying to tune itself in to the clearest frequency. I was being used like some sort of human transmitter. I would experience every emotion there is, all at the same time, and extreme fluctuations in body temperature sweeping over me.

A couple of weeks after the funeral I spent one particularly hot sunny day in Mum's back garden on the sun bed. The sky was clear blue, the ground arid and my mood better than usual. I felt more happy and relaxed than I had done in a long time.

Within the next few minutes I became aware that John was sitting at the foot of the bed. There was nothing to be seen with the naked eye, but the sensation was overwhelmingly powerful. Peace and harmony crept over me in an instant. I could almost see him, almost touch him, if it weren't for the invisible veneer between us.

Mum entered the garden, took one surprised look at me and said, 'He's here isn't he?'

'Yes,' I replied with a fluttering heartbeat.

'I thought so. I can pick up a very strong sensation of him somewhere in this area here,' she said as she moved her hands slowly through the space immediately in front of her.

'Me too,' I said. 'That's strange isn't it? That we can both sense something.'

'I know. Wait there a minute. I'm going to get the camera and take some photos. You just never know what might come out!'

'I hardly think so. He's not likely to show himself is he?'

'Well, you never know. Anyway, I'd like some pictures of you lying there like that. It's such a lovely day.'

Mum hurried back with the camera and began to click away. The whole time I felt he was sitting right there with me. I could feel the love as it emanated from the empty space in front of me, could almost see the daft expression on his face, and I felt incredibly happy.

Could he really be here with us? Was this really happening? Mum and I discussed the topic of life after death as we had done many times before in the past, and agreed it was feasible. The only thing she refused to believe was that objects could fly around the room on their own. She didn't believe in the poltergeist phenomenon. In the days to come, she'd be proved wrong over that too.

My next visit to my parents, the following morning, was interrupted by a loud crashing noise from the direction of the garden shed. I frowned at Mum, she frowned at me, and Dad was at a loss which direction to look in.

'What the hell was that?' I shouted.

'No idea,' Mum replied, as she nervously made her way towards the tiny brick-built building to investigate. After several minutes close inspection of the tool house, she concluded that there seemed to be nothing out of place.

Two days later Mum went into the shed again to find all Dad's tools on the floor, including some he hadn't used in years. She quizzed him about it. He had no more idea than her how it could have happened.

She continued to harp on about the funeral song. 'I must find out who it's by.'

'Why?'

'I don't know. I just get this feeling that we need to find out more about it. Aren't you interested at all?'

'No, not really. It was obviously John and Karen's song, nothing to do with me. Why would I want to listen to a song that reminded him of someone else?'

'You must know who sings it.'

'No, I don't. It's recent, that's all I know. I heard it not long ago.' I didn't know it then, but my comment in church about music being the link between us was starting to come true.

Before the week was out, I woke up in the middle of the night feeling restless. As I tossed and turned attempting to get back to sleep, I felt two taps on my left shoulder, turned over quickly to ask Robin what he was playing at, and noticed he was still fast asleep, and facing in the opposite direction.

Within seconds the words of a song began to play over and over inside my head, as if someone was putting them there. I knew this song was recent too, but I couldn't think what it was or who it was by. It had the refrain, 'you can make me whole again,' which was repeated without pause, spoken not sung, and wouldn't stop however hard I fought to clear my mind. The strange episode lasted for about 30 minutes.

In the morning I was determined to find out more about the song that had kept me awake. If anyone knew it my daughter would.

'It's on one of my compilation discs,' she said. I asked her to play it for me, and listened in astonishment as the words intertwined John's feelings and my own. Then I remembered how John frequently used to creep up behind me and tap me twice on the left shoulder. On turning round there'd be no one in sight, because he'd be standing on the opposite side, the right, rather than the left. He did it all the time, not just to me but to everyone. I'd never remembered it till now. My blood suddenly ran cold. The hand that I'd felt in the night, as real as my own, had been his. It had to be. But how was it possible?

When I told Mum of these strange experiences she was fascinated, but she'd also been having a few of her own. She could sense a permanent restlessness in the air.

'He's not happy, you know.'

'No?'

'No. I get the feeling things are not good. He's tormented.'

'Why?'

'I'm not sure. I just get that feeling.'

I suggested a trip to the supermarket, might break up the day, and take our minds off things for a while; and anyway we both needed to stock up on some groceries. As we browsed around the bread and cakes, the 'funeral song' came on over the store tannoy system.

'You know what that is, don't you?' Mum said anxiously.

'Yes, I know.'

'We must find out who it's by.'

Oh no, not this again; she was like a woman possessed, I thought. As it would turn out, I wasn't too far from the truth.

'Go and ask someone,' she continued.

'You must be joking,' I replied. 'I'm really not that interested.'

'Well, I will then.' She pulled up the first available assistant. 'The song that's just played. Who sings it?'

'David Gray' came the reply. 'It's lovely, isn't it? Very haunting. It's from his new album; we've got it on sale over there!' She pointed Mum in the right direction.

'Come on,' said Mum, 'let's take a look!'

133

Reluctantly, I trundled off to the music department, and scoured the D and G sections. 'Here it is!' I shouted. *White Ladder*. As soon as I laid eyes on it, I knew it was very John.

'Buy it!' Mum insisted.

'I can't buy something I've never listened to. I might not like any of the songs on it.'

'Well, I think you should buy it. Something's telling me you should.'

'I don't know. I'm not sure. I'll think about it.'

I took Mum home, and on my return the store seemed to beckon me inside for a second look. I deliberated and mused, as my restless feet paced backwards and forwards across the supermarket floor. The last time I had such strong sensations had been over the evening paper the night I learned of John's death. This time, I had to make the right choice. I was dubious but curiosity got the better of me. I picked it up and headed towards the checkout.

16

As soon as I got home, I needed to listen to the mysterious CD I'd been compelled to buy against my better judgement. Kneeling down on the floor, next to the hi-fi unit, I waited anxiously for the lyrics of the first song to bowl me over, and they did too. Fortunately I was already sitting down. If I'd been standing, I'd have been knocked off my feet. At the first words my mouth fell open in shock. I sat totally mesmerized, as phrases jumped out at me. This wasn't David Gray singing, it was John. John's voice was speaking to me through the words of the song.

Listen to 'Babylon'! came the voice in my head. *Listen and you'll understand!* I listened intently as instructed. I couldn't believe my ears. The tiny hairs on my arms were visibly erect, as those chilling and poignant words drifted purposefully towards me. As they penetrated my thoughts, sadness welled in my heart, and an invisible cloud of cold air materialized.

I sobbed and sobbed. Oh, dear God, it's not possible. These feelings weren't just his feelings, they were mine too. The words told me about many years of loneliness and despair. Of going to the football match on a Saturday and the enjoyment of the game marred by the desolation of a hollow spirit. Every phrase in the song paralleled his own experiences: his need to confess the bad mistakes he'd made. Jealousy, bitterness, and ridicule, were exactly what he'd heaped on me. In 'Sail Away' he told me how everything he'd held dear had vanished without trace. That was *me*, I'd vanished without trace. 'Say Hello, Wave Good-bye' told the story of our lives. Like ships that pass in the night, we had never really known one another, not properly, because we'd both spent our lives with other people. We had tried to make it work, me in a cocktail skirt, and him in a suit, but it just wasn't to be.

Every word was spot on to the last detail, summing up our years with and without each other. The *White Ladder* album could have been written for us, an epitaph to our tragic existence.

The one thing I could not bring myself to do was listen to the funeral song, 'This Year's Love'. For the time being I left it well alone. I couldn't get my head around any of this: two whole lifetimes of regret in one album.

I lent Mum the CD, told her to listen and give me her opinion.

'My God!' she said in bewilderment, 'it's about you and John. It's amazing. It's like the story of your lives. What the hell is going on here?'

'I don't know, but it's unbelievable isn't it?'

'Unbelievable?' she repeated, 'It's not this David Gray singing at all. It's as if John is singing it. Communicating through these songs.'

'I know, he is, isn't he? This isn't just my imagination, is it?'

'No, definitely not. I'm feeling it too. It's too incredible for words, but it *is* happening. He never got the chance to tell you how he felt and how much you meant to him while he was still alive, so he's telling you now, through these songs.'

'He really is, Mum, isn't he?'

'Yes, there's no doubt about it. It's all about you and him.'

'But do you realize what we're saying? We've got absolute proof of life after death! And why us? I mean this isn't normal is it? No one would ever believe this.'

'It certainly isn't normal. Perhaps things will become clearer to us in time.' It wasn't just the sentiment of the songs. The words were words that John would have used himself, words that he did use in the past when we discussed our problems.

Next morning I woke feeling restless and fidgety. I drifted pointlessly around the house like an abandoned puppy. What was wrong with me? I was unimaginably keyed up.

Within half an hour voices began to intrude my thoughts. *Play 'This Year's Love'*, I was instructed. I recognized the voice as John's and replied accordingly.

'It wasn't our song. It was yours and Karen's. I don't want to listen to something that reminds you of her.'

No, he replied insistently, *not for her, for you. It's for you listen!*

Once again I was compelled to act against my wishes. I sat down, cleared my mind and just listened to the words.

Tears flowed from my eyes; bitter-sweet memories took me back to a turbulent past. The song was a reference to all those impassioned nights we'd held each other beneath the street lamp outside my house, always so late at night. This song was directed at me after all. 'This year's love' was the love I was feeling for him in this, the year of his death. It was overwhelmingly sad. Suddenly the room became chilled. As the coldness intensified it seemed to tumble gently down my cheek. I could sense those eyes searing into mine as he observed my response throughout the following minutes. He was there. He was right there beside me and I wanted desperately to touch him. My hand reached out in vain. He swiftly veered to one side. His disembodied spirit had no more chance of blending with my deficient form, than I had of breaking free from my worldly shell and integrating with him, yet we were merged in our mutual suffering through those evocative words as they pulsated the room. He'd never really opened up to me in words, only in actions. Now, for the first time, they were forthcoming. For the very first time the spoken word was conveying what I always knew in my heart to be true.

Mum really isn't going to believe this I thought, I wanted to tell her straight away. Bursting with excitement I drove as fast as I could to her house, opened the front door and charged towards the kitchen. Before I had chance to say anything, Mum turned around very slowly, with disbelieving eyes.

'Oh, Amanda!' she said, 'I've had voices in my head all morning. *She was the only one! You've got to tell her, she was the only one!*'

I'd waited all my life to hear those words. 'You can't be serious. You as well? This is beyond everything.'

'And that song, "This Year's Love",' she continued, 'it wasn't for Karen, it was for you. It was directed at you!'

'No. It's just not possible is it? *Is it?*'

We both stood lost for words. How could it be that both of us had experienced voices the same morning, giving us similar messages? If I had any crumb of doubt before, surely there could be none now?

'What do you think the song means?' Mum asked.

'Not sure. Perhaps the love I'm feeling for him now in this year of his death.'

'No, you're wrong. It's the love he was feeling for you as he lay dying. He listened to the *White Ladder* album, this song in particular, realized that he'd searched everywhere, tried every-thing, and it was the love he felt for you that he wanted to last. He was desperately hoping that he could see you again to tell you how he really felt before it was too late. He wanted to put things right with you before he left this life, tell you how he really felt all that time. That's what it means.'

I had told Mum previously that I believed he'd died from AIDS. She wasn't shocked or surprised, and although we still had no concrete proof, she seemed to sense, just as I did, that it was true. 'You really believe that's what he died from?' she said.

'I couldn't be more sure about anything. I'm as certain as if I'd given it to him myself. Do you know what this means?'

'What?'

'Everything I ever believed has come true. All those feelings, those messages; just the way I always knew they would.'

'In the last moments of his life,' she continued, 'he was agitated and tormented beyond belief because you hadn't seen each other in so long. You picked up that anxiety. Through the words of David Gray's songs he's able to tell you what he was feeling. It's important that you listen carefully and you'll be able to build up a picture of his life without you.'

'Do you think I should see a spiritualist?'

'There's no need. I don't know why, but everything is coming through to me. I'm picking it all up as clear as anything. In the end so much will have happened you could write a book!'

At the time I didn't remember the voices that had told me on more than one occasion I would write about my life with John one day, enabling me to relive my memories and convey the truth about life after death.

I became obsessive about playing the *White Ladder* album. I'd be anxious to hear it again and again, then afterwards I'd feel calmer, more relaxed. At first 'This Year's Love' brought back images of the coffin lying solemnly in that packed church, but the more I listened, the more those images were replaced by that of two teenage lovers hugging each other for dear life beneath a council street lamp and a star-filled sky on a cold winter's night.

Then I found myself wandering into records shops on instruction. I'd be told exactly what to buy and what tracks to listen to. Each time I would argue with the silent voice. I could not purchase something I had not already heard, it was ludicrous, but the voices were insistent.

I had no idea what I was buying, yet as soon as I got home and listened to the requested tracks, I was astounded at how closely they related to our lives. It became apparent to me that from the very beginning, just after we'd split, he'd bitterly regretted the way things had turned out. Regret had haunted him until the last moment of his life, and even beyond it.

Some of the albums I bought were others by David Gray. All of them painted a picture of a very sad and lonely life, and made me realize that I'd done much worse to him, than he had to me. After all, he'd never married, never had children. He'd remained the more faithful, while I'd sold myself to the highest bidder and deprived him of all the things that were rightfully his. The songs told of needing to know if love was real, of painful memories, one-night stands and prostitutes. Of someone that hated himself, yet still felt a need to love and be loved by someone, anyone, even if only for one night. Of a person who had thrown away everything he'd ever wanted or cared about, and wished he could bring it back again, bring *me* back again. John's sentiments from 20 years before were repeated word for word. I could no longer contain my emotions. To the melodious sound of David Gray's guitar the tears dripped into my trembling coffee cup. 'Gathering Dust' was the song, and my heart shuddered to the last verse, and the most beautiful words ever written of love. Exactly how I remembered it.

Each time I drove past the cemetery, significant songs would start to play on the radio. From the first word emitted the feeling that John was conveying his thoughts to me was so intense. I'd be compelled to buy each one immediately and play it over and over. Once I'd listened and understood, any feelings of anxiety and restlessness would diminish. It was John's restlessness I was feeling, not my own. For a few minutes, it seemed, I was held under a magical spell that would only be broken when the song ended. I was absolutely bewitched. Lover's promises, broken hearts, jealousy, and then the most important phrase: 'the only thing I ever wanted was the feeling that . . . I was the only one you ever thought about.'

That's exactly how it was! He craved the love that only I could give him, and he was the only person I ever thought about. Those words that told me I would never know how much I'd hurt him brought tears to my eyes. I did know how much I'd hurt him.

These songs seemed to follow me wherever I went, in shops, on the radio at home, in the car. I'd cry out, 'What on earth is happening to me?' One day after leaving Mum's 'Babylon' came on the radio almost as soon as I set off. I rang Mum immediately and let her hear for herself.

'Can you believe this?' I screamed down my mobile.

'Not really, no. It's too incredible for words' came her shocked reply.

As we spoke she was interrupted by a loud bang from my old room. She ran upstairs and was stunned to see a milky white circular image in the bedroom window, about the size of a ball or a head. At first she thought her double-glazed sealed unit had broken down, but after 30 minutes the image vanished. Three weeks later the same thing happened downstairs, and like the previous time the shape disappeared within half an hour.

'What do you think of that?' she asked Dad.

'It's the ghost of Amanda's John, isn't it? He's here in this house with us!'

17

One month later we decided to take some flowers to the cemetery. Although it had been my original intention not to return, it now seemed I was being persuaded to change my mind. The red and white heart necklace John gave me had been symbolic for me, and I wanted to recreate that gesture, so I bought one bunch of white roses, one bunch of red, and intermingled them.

We were shocked by the scene that greeted us at the grave. It was completely bare. All the funeral flowers had gone, but no more had been left in their place. It looked sad and uncared for. I laid my flowers carefully at the top, and Mum placed a small posy just below.

'When Karen dropped her rose on the coffin at the funeral, she had to share that moment with everyone else. You have got him all to yourself. It's just you and him now, your private time together,' Mum said.

'Yes,' I replied, 'just us.'

She left us alone, and I knelt down to kiss the grave, and view the simple wooden cross that bore his name and untimely age of death.

'I'm sorry John.' The words spilled from my lips. 'I'm so, so, sorry. I never stopped loving you.' I knew instinctively he was watching and listening. 'Please forgive me.'

Warmth and serenity soothed my aching muscles and heavy heart. That candle had just been relighted inside me, and I was able to leave much less agitated than when I'd arrived.

Ever since the day I first listened to 'This Year's Love' these 'breeze' sensations had been gaining intensity. They were pretty constant. This cool breath of air seemed to hover purposefully over me, always caressing gently as it moved past my face. My first thought had been that I must be sitting in a draught, but it felt different somehow. It would occur in all sorts of different environments: shops, restaurants, outdoors, places where it would be impossible to feel a chill, and above all at Mum's house. It was forceful, loving, extraordinary. I *knew* it was him. I told Mum about the sensations.

'It must be lovely,' she said.

'It is,' I said. 'It's him. I know it's him.'

'That's real love, that is' she said. 'Real love!'

'Well, it always was.'

'You know his presence is particularly strong in this room, and in the bedroom?' Mum asked.

'Is it?'

'He was happy here. Happier than anywhere else. More than in his own home.'

'They're the two rooms where we spent most of our time together, that must be why. The happiest days of his life were spent in this house, as mine were. He's come back to where the memories are.'

Mum couldn't experience the breezes, but we both encountered days of agitation, and days of calmness. On the calm days, nothing significant would happen. We'd feel relaxed and subdued. On other days we'd be filled with anxiety and restlessness. John would be trying to convey a message. Each time, the build-up was the same. I'd be wound up for about half an hour, then the voices would begin. They'd come through loud and clear. Sometimes Mum would get the messages, and I'd just encounter the restlessness, or it might be the other way round. Sometimes we'd both receive the messages at the same time. Discussions would take place between the three of us.

'Why don't I feel these breezes that Amanda speaks of?' Mum asked.

Because we weren't lovers! came the reply.

'I should hope not, John,' Mum said.

'I should hope not!'

Though the breezes eluded her, she was able to sense a warm pressure around the shoulders. 'He puts his arm around me sometimes,' she told me. 'I can feel the weight of his arm on me, trying to give me comfort.' I'd felt this once or twice too; a warm, pressing sensation.

Electrical equipment began to take on a mind of its own, at Mum's house, mine, and at work too. Paper would go up and down in the printer several times if I tried to print anything. I'd say, 'Stop messing around, John, I'm busy,' and the paper would promptly obey and move down into the machine. For weeks and weeks every time I depressed the letter F, it would fail to show on screen until I'd pushed it three times in succession. I sensed this was some sort of hidden message. After much deliberation it suddenly came to me, like a bolt of lightning: it was 'Forgive'. John wanted me to forgive him. Of course I forgave him, that was the easy part. It was myself I had difficulty in pardoning. My need for forgiveness was surely greater than his. Once I convinced him of that, the letter F, and the computer, gave me no more problems.

I needed to try and find out more about the things that were happening to us, so I took myself off to the local library. To my surprise, they had quite a selection of books on life after death, so I grabbed a couple from the shelf, and began to read. Soon I was reading about the things that were happening to me. First I discovered that during a seance the primary sensation experienced when the departed person is close by is a series of 'cool breezes'. Next, that after death the spirit takes on a 'new body', which is spherical in shape, rather like a globe or a ball, and that when a spirit travels from one dimension to another, the sound barrier may be broken. I remembered Mum's milky white circular image in the window, and the loud bang she'd heard just before entering the room.

Then I read an article describing out-of-body experiences and the same sequence of events leading up to spiritual expulsion that I had remembered having as a five-year-old. How could a child of five know anything of how to induce such a transition? The only way I could have known was if the knowledge was procured sometime in my past.

From a book on near-death experiences I discovered that communication is made from one spirit to another using a form of telepathy, just as Mum and I had been experiencing, John's thoughts inside our own heads. I read the words again and again. If I'd read this article sometime before, I might have retained it in my subconscious, but I had read about this after the event. There was just no explanation. And surely for two people to hear the same messages ruled out the possibility that one of them might be cracking up? There had never been any telepathy between Mum and me before.

'He's in your head all the time, isn't he?' Mum would say, and that's exactly how it was. He was inside our heads, and had access to our private thoughts constantly.

Later in the week I was walking in the town centre when I spotted Jeeves in the distance.

Tell him! said John. I suddenly became aware that he was standing right behind me, behind my left shoulder. There was no doubt in my mind of his presence, just like the day in Mum's garden.

As Jeeves came closer, I braced myself to mutter the words I could hardly believe. 'John died, you know.' My voice trembled so much I could hardly speak.

'Oh no!' he replied. 'I just can't believe it!'

'He was only thirty-seven,' I continued.

'My God,' said Jeeves. 'It's so unbelievable. Here's me nearly seventy and still going strong. It doesn't seem fair does it? It must be hitting you really hard. After all, you two were so close!'

We still are, said John's silent voice, as Jeeves began to walk away.

I wanted to shout after him, 'Jeeves, we still are!' But he'd have thought me crazy. If I was having trouble believing it, then no one else could possibly understand. I would have loved to have been able to tell someone, anyone. It was far too important to keep to myself. I was bursting to break this wonderful news, that life after death really does exist, without any doubt. Keeping it all in was, and still is, one of the hardest things. But how would I convince others if I tried?

Where are you going? John would ask me sometimes, or *What are you doing?* The breezes and the strong sense that he was with me would always precede conversation. As soon as he'd made his presence known the voices would begin in my head, usually when I least expected them. Perhaps when I was being served in a shop or a bank, for example, and often when I had my mind on something else, he would suddenly interrupt my thoughts.

I'd receive instructions to visit the grave. I didn't think it was a good idea myself, but he'd remain insistent. I always found that if he asked anything of me it had to be done there and then. There was never any question of ignoring or denying the request. I felt compelled to do whatever he asked, even if it was something I wasn't too sure of myself. His wishes it seemed were my commands. Some days I'd arrive at Mum's and she'd say 'We've got to visit the grave today.' I'd feel it too, an overwhelming compulsion that had to be acted on immediately.

If I bought some flowers for home, he'd say, *Where's mine?* So the next time I went shopping I'd buy some for the grave Even the colours were chosen by him. One such time he insisted on some white roses, so I made a determined search through the display. There weren't any white roses, or so I believed.

There is one bunch left. Look for it!

'No, John, there isn't. I've looked and looked; there aren't any white ones anywhere. They must have all gone.'

Keep looking, he continued.

There's one bunch left. Just keep looking and you'll find it.

In a state of mental confusion I continued to grapple with the endless tightly-wrapped packages, and suddenly there it was, the last bunch of white roses, just as he'd told me they would be, and I smiled.

Told you! he added. I gave a faint laugh, though I realized I was probably on camera giggling to myself, no doubt the talk of the staff room – the halfwit in the fresh flower aisle who keeps smiling and blushing for no apparent reason.

When I tried to pay for my shopping at the checkout, a blast of cool air suddenly rushed up beside me. *Remember 'Humphrey Davey'?* I could hardly breathe for a second. The words took me back to that London cab ride in 1982. It was one memory I had not recalled in a long time; something he used to say to me repeatedly in the months following that day – 'Remember Humphrey Davey?' – knowing that it would set me off laughing helplessly.

Over the next few months more and more lost thoughts would come back to me, things that he said, ways that he touched me, little intimate things I'd forgotten all about. With their return came a vividness as sharp as if it had happened yesterday. Mum felt the same. She said she could see John serving on the ticket counter at work or walking down the aisle to call the main session, as if it had only just happened.

'Don't you find that everything is so sharp?' she said. 'Sharper than it ever was?'

'Yes,' I'd reply, 'unbelievably so. You know, so much is coming back to me with every passing day, I get the feeling that soon there won't be a single thing I don't remember. The fact that he has the ability to put certain thoughts inside my head is truly magnificent.'

I began to wonder just how much access he did have to my private thoughts and feelings. Would I ever again have a truly private moment? What a strange situation I now found myself in. I could be viewed for 24 hours a day from all angles. He was able to see me when I looked my best and when I looked my worst. Did he follow me to the toilet? There were times there, too, when I'd feel his graceful and ubiquitous presence; although I found that if I told him to wait outside he'd usually do as I asked, or so I would think.

Robin began to suspect that strange things were going on. The atmosphere was frequently charged and tense. As John's presence grew stronger, my love and affection was re-kindled, and my relationship with Robin began to wane. I'd become a teenager again, excited and starry-eyed just like the first time, keen for the start of each new day and the unforeseen events it would bring.

One night we were awoken from our sleep by a noise, as if the window had been left open and papers were being blown about in the breeze. There were loud rustling and shuffling sounds, and a feeling that we were most definitely not alone.

Robin sat bolt upright in bed and shouted, 'there's someone in the room! What's going on?'

'It's all right,' I replied calmly. 'I think I must have left the window open and the wind is blowing things about.'

I knew exactly what it was, or rather who, but I could hardly tell Robin, who didn't believe in 'that crap', as he called it.

18

Mum and I continued to discuss the things that were happening to us. It was all we could speak of; the other things in our lives felt very insignificant.

We both found that sometimes we would ask John a question but receive no answer; at other times, he would respond with the answer before we'd finished asking. The voices that we heard were distinctly separate from our own thoughts. Often they would seem to be coming from a great distance.

'One day, when it's wet and dark, I'm going to see him,' she said. 'I'm going to see him exactly as he was, the full image. I don't know why I should think that. I've really got no idea, but I just know that I will see him, without a doubt.'

'Why do you think that we haven't seen him already?'

'He hasn't been dead long enough.'

'That's coming through to me too. It's too soon.'

Mum started to tell me about a dream she'd had the night before. Apparently I was in a terrible state. John was just standing there watching. 'Look what you've done to her!' Mum told him. 'You're supposed to be looking after her. Look at the state you've let her get into! I've never seen her like that before, she's absolutely shattered!' All the while he never spoke, just watched and listened, as he had done in my last dream. We weren't sure what it meant, but more dreams were soon to follow, and each one would prove stranger than the one before.

Some days I'd be enveloped by a feeling of euphoria because he was so close, and there were other times when depression hung over me like a great cloud. I'd be only too aware of what I'd lost, that I'd never again be able to have a conversation with him, or see the expressions on his face. He was still with me, he'd proved that beyond doubt, yet we were literally worlds apart. It was hard for me to accept that the physical body I had touched and held and kissed and made love with, lay decomposing beneath the ground, and that I would never again, in this life anyway, be able to hold or touch that physical form. I could have kicked myself a thousand times over for not being there when it mattered, and for not making contact sooner, for letting so many years pass by without exchanging a word. I had had the power to make it happen, but didn't. This person was the other half of me and we'd lived most of our lives without each other. It had been 13 years since I last saw his face. Everyone that had been part of his life had seen him more recently than I had. It was ridiculous. How could two people who loved each other as much as we did, force themselves to stay apart for so long?

In May we would go on holiday. It had been booked for some considerable time before John's death, and although I'd previously been looking forward to our tour of Canada and the States, it was the last thing on my mind now. I had a longing to stay close to my home town. I needed to be close to John's grave, close to my old house, the epicentre of these supernatural occurrences, and close to my past. Mum said that she'd visit the cemetery during my absence and look after him for me. That gave me some peace of mind.

Just before landing in New York, 'This Year's Love' started to play on the in-flight radio. Within three hours of arrival I heard two more David Gray songs; my daughter said they seemed to be following me around. John wanted me to know he was there with me, that he'd be with me wherever I went.

The 'breeze' continued relentlessly throughout the holiday. I'd be sitting in a bar chatting with Robin about the events of the day when that familiar rush of air would suddenly begin to swirl around me, radiating love and sensuality as it floated serenely past. Has Mum visited the grave yet? I wondered to myself. *She has* came the reply.

True enough, on my return home Mum told me that she'd been two days before, my question had been answered. However, she wasn't happy; she'd undergone a restless and disturbing time while I'd been away.

'You wouldn't believe the things that have been happening to me,' she said. 'Am I glad you're back home!'

I listened to what she had to tell me. 'Someone had left a plant on the grave. There was a green ribbon on it bearing John's name. Some green stones had been placed around it in a circle. I recognized this symbol, because I'd seen it before in Scotland. It's a Celtic sign, representing the unbroken circle of life. I knew straight away what it meant. I came out of that graveyard in a trance. She went on, 'Do you want to see the photos? The ones I took of you in the garden, before you went away – the day we first felt that John was with us?' She threw them down on the dining room table in front of me. 'Just look! Just look at that!'

Every photo was a complete blank; every one numbered, and every one clear. In all my life I don't ever remember Mum taking one bad photo, let alone a whole film. If there was one thing Mum could do well, it was take photos.

'What do you think?' she asked. 'When I collected the film from Boots, the lady told me that this is most unusual. She could think of no reason why the film hadn't developed, except that a fault in the camera, so she sent it away to be checked. It was in perfect working order, nothing wrong with it at all. The film also appeared to be faultless. As soon as I got home, John's voice said to me, *I'm still here, and I can do things that you can't do!* What can you say about that? I just don't know what to say or what to think any more. He's been so agitated while you were away, but he's happier now you're back. There's something else I don't know if I should tell you.'

'What is it?' I asked.

'I had an upsetting conversation with him. It was so sad I could have wept.'

'Tell me what was said. I have to know.'

'It was the day I got back from the grave. I was standing in the kitchen by the sink, when he spoke to me: *Amanda broke my heart!* I said, "You broke hers." *I made mistakes*, he said, and I said "So did she." *But I died for my mistakes.* "And Amanda lives with hers." *Yes, but one day, one day!*

The anguish was apparent on her face. 'Amanda this is so, so sad.'

'You don't need to tell me. I've lived with this for nearly twenty years, and now I have to live with the outcome of my actions. The guilt and the pain will never leave me.'

'I knew that you two were close, that John was the great love of your life, but never imagined anything on this scale,' Mum said.

'Well, now you know.'

'But you never said anything in all this time.'

'I kept it inside.'

'It's tragic that we can't change any of this.'

'I know. I still keep thinking it's a bad dream. That I'll wake up and discover that he's not really dead after all, but I know I'm not going to.'

We were keen to know if these incidents would cease over time, or if they would continue indefinitely. Why was Mum involved, anyway? The only thing that came to me was that Mum had been involved in every decision regarding John. When I was a little girl she told me to keep my hair long because men generally preferred it that way, and John certainly did. It had been through her that I'd first started work at the bingo hall. She'd sanctioned John's first visit to our home. She'd been the one who'd told me to give him a second chance, to enjoy ourselves and make the most of things while we were young, as if she could see into the future. In fact, she had always been there with me, protecting me, in a way John always saw her as a force to be reckoned with in order to get close to me. She had brought us together. She had been the one to inform me of John's death, but the three of us were linked by much more than just these things. We seemed to be on the same wavelength. Despite John's frequent jibes at Mum we'd retained a special bond.

'John seemed to be genuinely afraid of me,' she said. 'Why was that, do you think? I know I used to speak to him in my strict, stern voice, but he knew I never meant it really.'

'Yes,' I replied. 'And you knew he never meant it when he used to come out with those sarcastic comments about old witches.'

'I know, it was all in good fun. But seriously, he always had a way of looking at me, as if he could see something beyond, something to be really wary of.'

'That's the way we looked at each other too. We could always see something more than what was visible on the surface. It was like going back hundreds of years.'

'I think we'll get used to this,' she said. 'I think one day it'll just seem normal. It will become a normal part of our lives.'

For quite some time I'd been having trouble with a Mirena coil, and the family planning clinic advised me to go to hospital to try and find out why. Mum offered to come with me. My appointment was three months to the day after John's death, at the same time of his death, a quarter to three, and I was to find myself in the same department he might have attended, the department for sexually transmitted diseases. I was somewhat perturbed to be in such a place; I'd only had one sexual partner in 17 years and that was my husband. I was assured the procedure was purely routine. As I entered the hospital, I began to feel unwell and edgy. John's life had ebbed away in that building and I was feeling it. As we sat waiting for my results, Mum said she was beginning to hear voices. 'I think I'm picking up the last moments of his life;' she said, staring in amazement. 'I don't know what's happening to me, I don't know what's happening!' she repeated over and over in a confused manner, then 'He's here with us now.'

'Is he?'

'He says he's behind the plant.' There was a large plant to our right.

Before I had chance to think, I was called back in to the examination room. All my tests were clear; my problems had been caused merely by the end of the coil's lifespan. On my return, Mum informed me that she'd observed John following me down the corridor, a smoky white image floating obediently behind me. It crossed my mind that I was having to encounter all the same things that he had at the hospital.

A couple of weeks later, I returned to the family planning clinic to have my replacement coil fitted. I was a little apprehensive, as the first time had been quite uncomfortable. As always, John was with me. *Are you OK?* he asked.

'I'm fine. Just a bit nervous.' Nervous of the insertion itself, and the fact that John was about to see me in a most uncompromising position with my legs splayed out wide, for the first time in years. The first coil was inserted but got caught on something, and came out of place. The second coil wouldn't open properly following insertion, so a third coil had to be used. The nurse told me she'd never encountered such a thing in all her nursing years. Three coils had to be used in one go, at great cost to the NHS. She asked me to keep quiet – if the powers that be were to hear of such a thing, she'd be in trouble, though it had been no one's fault, just a crazy fluke.

For some reason since John's death the number three had been continually cropping up in my life. It wouldn't be long before I was to find out why.

By the end of the month I'd been getting used to the breeze sensations. I'd tried and tried in vain to see something, strained my eyes to the limit, yet I'd never seen the faintest hint of anything. I had no reason to think that June 30th would be any different. I'd been watching television all evening, and the breeze had been circling around me as usual. Robin was sitting opposite with his nose firmly in the newspaper and I turned my gaze away to reply to something he'd said. When I turned my head back to the television, I froze rigid. There was a white cloud of vapour slowly rising before me, which gradually dispersed before my eyes

'Oh my God!' I shouted.

'What's wrong with you?' Robin asked raising his head for a moment.

'Nothing. I just took a funny turn for a minute, but I'm all right now.'

John's voice came into my head on cue: *Did I frighten you?*

'No. I was just startled. Wasn't expecting to see anything. You took me by surprise. It was you wasn't it?'

Yes, it was me.

I couldn't believe my ears, or my eyes. What I had seen was as clear and as real as anything could be, as real as anything else in the room; a cloud of no definite shape, but with more density than a cloud of smoke or steam, and with more controlled movement.

The image wouldn't leave my head. It's one thing to say that you believe in ghosts, and one thing to recall being able to leave your physical body, but actually to see the spirit of someone you knew well in life, to know without any doubt that although their body lies decomposing in a box beneath the ground, they continue to exist, is utterly astounding, beyond comprehension. This was proof of another life, life beyond the grave. I felt honoured and privileged in a way I couldn't explain. I wanted to tell Robin the truth, wanted to tell everyone that I had proof. How on earth could I keep this a secret? It seemed far too exciting to keep to myself, but deep down I knew that's exactly what I had to do, at least for the time being. Robin certainly wouldn't have believed me, anyway. Who would have believed it? It was just too fantastic to be true, but it WAS true. Mum would understand; at least I could tell her, but she wasn't so amazed. Following my hospital appointment that day, she'd continued to see clouds of vapour regularly drifting in and out of various rooms in the house.

'One time, I was on the phone to your sister,' she said, 'when he drifted through from the porch, leaving me speechless. I see him in the hall and the living room and the bedroom, and sometimes your dad tells me I look as if I've just seen a ghost!'

'You know, sometimes, I say something to Robin, and I think to myself, where did I get that saying from? Then it comes back to me, a phrase John would use. Then I'll know that he's sitting in front of me laughing the way he used to, trying to make me laugh. He DOES make me laugh, and it's like turning the clock back twenty years! The other night I stood at the foot of the stairs and shouted the girls down for tea. *Wake the dead up, why don't you?* He said, making me giggle out loud. Just like him to say something like that!

There'll be times when I open the kitchen cupboard and this tremendous surge of air rushes out at me, or I might turn to walk across a room and bump right into him. This vast, powerful blast of cold air will almost knock me off my feet I even find myself apologizing when I walk into him. The front door slams shut on days when there's no wind, the video's taken on a mind of it's own, and as for the CD player! It's never worked properly, sometimes just won't play certain tracks. John tells me *It'll play today. Try one more time. this time it will play,* and it always does!'

'It's much the same here,' Mum said, 'The other day I walked into the front room and this milky white image suddenly appeared in my full-length mirror. *Me and Amanda, we messed each other around something terrible* he said, *but she carried things too far by marrying someone else.* "You could have married her. You had just as much chance to marry her as Robin did," I told him. *But I had no choice.* "That's rubbish" I said, "of course you had a choice. Everyone has a choice!" *But I didn't. I never had a choice, and I didn't realize what I had until I'd lost it! The day I left this house for the last time I would have given anything if she'd run after me, but she didn't.* I asked him who was doing this, him or God; and why me? *It's both,* he replied, *because you believe!* With that remark the conversation ended and the image disappeared.'

Before the month was out Mum went to Peterborough for the day. She'd taken plenty of money to spend, yet from the moment she arrived she was overcome by a compelling need to return home. After wandering around in a daze for about half an hour, swamped by feelings of uneasiness, she decided to call it a day. When she returned her first port of call was the bedroom, where she was greeted by a greyish-outlined head-and-shoulders phantom.

Where have you been? the figure asked.

'I've been to Peterborough to do some shopping' she replied.

You should be here! Amanda's here when you're here!

'That's silly, John.'

No it's not. It's not silly.

'Anyway, what are you doing here?'

I belong here.

'No you don't, John, this wasn't your home.'

I belong here. We belong here.

'Why do you keep appearing to me like this? Why don't you show yourself to Amanda; she wants to see you?'

One day when the time is right she'll see me, but not until then. One day in paradise.

'But you did show yourself to her a few weeks ago, she told me that she saw you.'

I shouldn't have done that. I broke the rules.

'What do you mean you broke the rules?'

I told you, I broke the rules.

The image vanished, leaving Mum even more shocked and surprised than ever. When she told me of this conversation things started to make more sense than they had done previously. Now it seemed I would see him again properly before I died, just as I had always been led to believe, probably at the point of my own death. It had never occurred to me that when I did see him again, he'd already be dead.

I was deeply touched that John had defied God himself in allowing me to see him. It was so very typical of him.

Even after this, I still had great difficulty getting my head around the many strange things that were happening on virtually a day-to-day basis. These things just don't happen to other people.

Why should they be happening to me? Or maybe they do happen to others, but they're just not talked about, for fear of ridicule. People should come forward to tell of their experiences. It's the only way we can learn the truth.

19

A few days later, I arrived at Mum's to find she'd been having another eventful morning.

'Can't you hear that noise?' she said. There was a horrendous commotion coming from the back garden.

'Yeah, what is it?'

'There's a raven sitting on my roof. Been there all morning making that ridiculous noise. Won't go away and it won't shut up. You do know it's the death bird, don't you? Go and have a look! My neighbour came out earlier to ask what was wrong with it because it sounded so demented.'

I stepped outside to take a look, craned my neck and stared at the squawking creature. Its gaze lowered and rested on my own startled eyes. The noise ceased immediately. A calm hush descended and within seconds it was gone.

'It couldn't have gone!' Mum shouted from the kitchen. 'We've been trying to shift it for hours. You know, it's something to do with John, isn't it? He's not happy today.'

'Why not?'

'Realization is setting in that he's dead, that he can't come back and be with you like he did before, but he feels a bit better now that you've come. He likes you being here.'

'Does he?'

'Well, he's with you all the time, he told me that, but he doesn't feel comfortable in your home, not like here. All the memories are here. This is where you and he spent your happiest days. Part of you both will always be here. Your home is filled with all the things that you and Robin have bought together. It's a strange environment for him. I've kept this house pretty much the same as when you knew him so it feels safe and familiar. He's told me you're not to feel sad any more. Says he knows how you feel. What happened to him was terrible, but that was then, this is now. That time is gone, and he's OK. You're not to feel sad.'

'Easier said than done,' I replied, 'I can't help but feel sad.'

'I told him how often we reflect on the happy times we spent together. Then I told him that this can't go on. You're married, and you've got a family to think about. *I know, I know* he answered.'

'Don't drive him away, Mum,' I pleaded. 'I couldn't face losing him again. It's been too long.'

'But the situation is impossible. He's gone for ever!'

He came back. He came back to be with me. I always knew he would. Sandra told me once that he'd realize it was me he really loved and that he'd come back, and he has. We need each other. We need to be together, really we do!'

That night I tossed and turned in bed, struggling to make sense of it all, going over the things I could have said and done. I wanted to put right all the wrong, start over again, but it was too late. Within seconds I could sense that John was standing next to the bed.

'I'm so sorry, John, really I am.'

So you should be! he replied, flippantly.

'I really am though.'

Sorry isn't good enough.

'I know, I know. I need your forgiveness.'

You have it. You've given me yours despite everything.

'I wish I could take back all the stupid things I said. If I could have one wish now I'd wish you back in my arms. All those arguments over a ring – how selfish and petty-minded. I've got my band of gold and it means nothing, not without you. You came back to me from beyond the grave because this is where your heart lies. That means far more than any ring. For the first time in my life now I can see what really matters.'

I'm sorry, too, that I ever let you go. With those words he departed.

Next day Mum was in more of a distressed state than I'd ever seen her before, trembling all over, her arms covered in goosepimples.

'Amanda, something horrible happened to me last night.'

'What on earth was it? You look awful.'

'I feel awful. I was getting ready for bed, turned around and stepped on a black dog cowering in front of me. I jumped back in surprise and it shrieked with fear as it slithered out of the bedroom door on its hind legs. I was too scared to venture out of the room to see where it went.'

'You're talking about a *ghost* dog?'

'Yes. But the worst thing of all was the noise it made. It made the same noise that a real dog would if I'd shouted at it for being naughty. It whimpered and slithered away making a scratching noise across the wooden floor as it left. It was horrible.'

'It couldn't have been John in another form?'

'No I don't think so. Everything we've experienced so far has been good, but this wasn't. This was evil. I'm worried it might come back.'

She had every right to be worried. I was too. It might appear to me next. The following day I tried to take my mind off things by doing some work in the garden. It was sunny and warm. Everything had been calm and quiet. All of a sudden there was a loud fracas between some birds, which resulted in one flying directly into my living room window. It stunned itself and landed on its back in the bushes below. Without hesitation I made my way across the lawn to see if there was any chance it had survived, picked it up very carefully and held it in the palm of my hand. 'Please don't die' I kept saying. 'Please don't die!'

The tiny fledgling's eyes became fixed on my own. It stared intently. I'd seen that look before. 'Is it you John? Is it really you?'

John's spirit seared into me. I was held several seconds in a trance, then the spell was broken. The creature spread wide its fluffy wings and propelled itself towards the heavens.

161

Once I'd recovered from the shock, I phoned Mum – she'd have something to say about it. Oddly enough, my dad answered the call; he rarely answered the phone if Mum was at home.

'Mum's cut her finger badly,' he said. 'She's too dizzy to get up. It's really quite bad, she's almost severed it.'

'When did this happen?' I asked suspiciously.

'About ten minutes ago,' came the reply. I looked at my watch. It had been ten minutes since the bird crashed into my window. It had to have been John. He'd tried to tell me what had happened.

I jumped into the car and went to Mum's aid. She needed an operation, and it was during her overnight stay in hospital that she encountered yet another unusual episode.

When she came home, she told me all about a strange conversation that had taken place with one of the other patients on the same ward.

'What's your name, then?' one old lady asked.

'Eleanor,' Mum replied.

'You don't look like an Eleanor to me. You look like a Hilda. I get the feeling I should call you Hilda. And there's a black dog sitting next to your bed.'

The other patients began to snigger – there was obviously no black dog near Mum's bed – all except Mum herself, who didn't find the comment so farfetched.

'You all think I'm silly,' the old lady said, 'but I tell you there's a black dog sitting in the corner to your right. It's as clear as anything.'

Later Mum asked the nurses if this woman was of sound mind.

'She might be old,' they said, 'but she's certainly not stupid.'

Mum looked at me blankly. 'What can you say about that? A black dog for goodness sake! Not by anyone else's bed, just mine. Is that a coincidence? And wanting to call me Hilda. My mother's name was Hilda. Was that just a coincidence? What could that woman see that no one else could? Things seem to be getting weirder by the minute.'

After telling me about this incident, Mum said 'This black dog, it frightens me. We're getting caught up here in things we shouldn't know anything about.'

'You're wrong,' I told her, 'we obviously are meant to know about them, or they wouldn't keep happening to us. We just need to educate ourselves. We need more information.'

The only thing I knew of black dogs from my accumulated knowledge of witchcraft, was that the devil himself can appear as such a creature, but surely that didn't bear thinking about? God is a three-letter word. Read in reverse it spells dog. Was it possible then that the black dog could be black God? Satan? If so, what was he doing in Mum's bedroom? Had the evil I sensed there as a child been driven away by the power of love generated by John and me? Or was it something else? The intensity of our love could prove a huge threat. Were we being studied and observed, perhaps? I tried not to think too much about it. It's not something that you want to delve too far into, or that you want to play on your mind, though a library book I perused at the time did confirm that Satan cannot project an animal in perfect form. The image will always appear to be flawed in some way, like a cat with no tail for example. Or a dog with no front legs? Mum's description of a dog slithering away on its hind legs only, came to mind. And doesn't the devil himself slither and slide like a serpent? We could only hope and pray for this incarnation to keep its distance.

Meanwhile John continued to make contact with both of us. My conversations with him centred around him asking me why I'd married someone else, and me asking him why he'd let me marry someone else. There were times when I'd get angry, times when I felt cheated out of the life I should have had. Angry with him for wasting his life, and for not telling me how he felt until it was too late. For not listening to me in the past, when I'd been so sure we were meant for one another. He'd have unsettled days too. Never be angry, just pensive and sad.

Amanda did it to me not once, but twice, he told Mum. *Got engaged to one person, then married another.*

We would have our fallings out. I'd express my hurt and my disappointment, tell him to leave me alone. Sometimes he would, for a few hours, then make a dramatic comeback, by telling me he didn't want to lose me again. On one occasion I remember particularly well, I was in the kitchen preparing the family's tea, and John was trying to discuss things with me, but I wasn't having any of it. I wasn't in a good frame of mind. It was one of my angry days.

I'll ruin your curry! he said cheekily. 'You wouldn't dare!' I replied. *Wouldn't I?*

Afterwards, I went upstairs to run a bath. As I pushed the door closed, he chirped in again, *Closing the door isn't going to keep me out!* I couldn't help but laugh out loud, as I gazed adoringly into the space immediately in front of me. We were smiling together. I just wished that I could see him.

'What's it like?' I asked, 'your new world?'

It's good. You'll like it. It's a bit strange at first, but it's good.

'But what's it really like? Tell me, I'd like to know.'

A world much like this one, only better.

'Do you see other people?'

I see many things.

'Do you miss being alive?'

Not really. I miss being with you properly.

'What do you do each day? How do you spend your days and nights?' No answer. 'You can't tell me, can you?' No answer.

I understand that there are certain things I cannot know about yet, some things I don't understand no matter how hard I try; like the time I was leaving Mum's to go to the nearby supermarket.

Don't leave! John insisted. *Please don't leave.*

'I have to, John. I've got things to do. I've got some shopping to get, then I have to go home.

'He doesn't want you to leave,' Mum confirmed.

'I know, he's just told me.'

As I was about to get into the car, Mum shouted over to me.

'Tell Amanda No, he says, I've to tell you No.'

164

'No to what?'

'He says not there, here. Tell Amanda here!'

'I don't understand.'

Did he mean not my house, but Mum's? I couldn't work it out.

John's desire to view me again through other's eyes was intensifying. On my next visit to Mum's, I was bowled over once again by his penetrating gaze, this time through the eyes of a dog. Just before I pulled up outside, I became aware of the creature running zestfully on the pavement opposite. Suddenly it stopped dead and froze rigid, as my car slowed to a halt. It looked in my direction, staring long and hard into my eyes, then crossed the road, sat down and waited patiently for me to get out. I opened the door and hurriedly made my way through the garden gate, closing it firmly behind me. It followed, sat down once again, tilted its head to one side and continued to scrutinize me from behind the railings. My eyes became transfixed with those of the animal. It seemed as if it were under some kind of magical spell, or was it me that was under the spell? My gaze was held, stuck fast, as was that of the dog. The windows of the soul reflected not that of a dumb animal, but the other half of myself. I was gazing upon my own spirit. The last time I'd looked into a pair of eyes with such tender warmth, until the episode with the bird, had been 13 years before when I looked into John's eyes for the last time. They'd drawn me like a magnet, just as these were drawing me now.

My niece, who was staying with Mum at the time, ran out from the house shouting, 'Look Nanny! Look at this dog staring at Auntie Amanda. Nanny look! It's just staring at her.'

It was the most amazing feeling. There was a tremendous surge of energy being transmitted from this animal into me. A few more magical seconds then I was dragged unwillingly back into the real world. I stepped indoors and it was all over. The animal ran away leaving me with an overwhelming sense of calm. That all too familiar 'déjà vu' and a hint of disbelief at what I'd just witnessed.

There had now been three incidents involving black dogs. That was our biggest clue to date: the number three.

20

For a while now I'd begun to feel more than just the breezes around me. John was able to let me feel his delicate touch. With the softest possible sensation I could feel his fingers caress my face and hair, with particular attention to the nose, like being stroked by a feather or a single strand of hair. Sometimes it felt as if foam-bath bubbles were disintegrating on my skin, or as if an insect was moving quickly over me.

Each night while watching television, the cool breezes would swirl, and his loving hands would examine the contours of my face. There'd be a falling sensation down my forehead or through my eyelashes, arousing my skin seductively as it glided past. My hair would tickle my ears as he moved through it. He had the ability to climb high into my nostrils with a tickling sensation if he was in a playful mood, making me laugh out loud or even jump up with a start. When in a more earnest state of mind, the cloud of chilled vapour would just radiate love as it settled and kissed me tenderly, becoming colder with increase in passion, and always stirring the hidden fires deep within my soul. I felt selfish absorbing all this pleasure that was being constantly bestowed, being unable to reciprocate in any way. I found myself in a permanent state of arousal whenever he was with me, which seemed to be most of the time. Instinctively, I'd know where-abouts he was in the room. I could just sense it. I would know immediately that I was gazing into his well-concealed eyes, and that they in turn were penetrating mine. Sometimes I wouldn't be too sure where he was. He'd play hide-and-seek, remain elusive, touch me in one place, then quickly move somewhere else just to fool me.

The only way I could try and show him any affection was by blowing kisses. This I would do frequently. Now and again I would be spotted, as my starry eyes smiled lovingly into space, or as I grinned in amusement at something he'd said. They all thought I was mad, but I couldn't tell them the real reason I was smiling like the Mona Lisa. Maybe that's why her face holds so much mystery. Maybe she too, was experiencing sensations from another world.

It was so hard to keep silent. Robin and the girls suspected something strange was going on, and they'd observe intently. I began to feel like a caged animal in a zoo. My every move was monitored and analysed.

'John, this is all so wonderful. You being here with me like this. It's amazing. I just wish I could have the other half of you.'
You are the other half of me, he replied.
'That's a lovely thing to say, really lovely'
It's true.
'I wish that I could see you, and hold you, and kiss you.'
One day. One day soon.
'Why not now?'
Because it's not time.
'I still can't believe that you've gone, that you're really dead.'
I'm not.
'I know, you know what I mean. How do we move forward now?'
One day at a time. Together.
'Yes, but it's so hard.'
Hard for me too, being here without you.
'I can't believe it. You were such a lovely person.'
I still am. I laughed out loud to that remark.
'What about Karen?'
What about her?

'You must have loved her. Everyone believed that you did. She believed that you did.'

Appearances aren't always what they seem. Wouldn't people say that you and Robin are happily married?

'Yes, point taken.'

I didn't love her. She made more of it than it really was. We were just friends. I was dying and needed someone, anyone. I didn't want to be alone. Can you understand?

'I understand. Did you make love with her?' I held my breath for a second in anticipation of his answer.

Yes.

My heart began to thump and nausea swept over me in an instant. It was hard not to feel jealousy. She had been there with him at the end of his life. I hadn't. At least I'd known him at a time when he was young and healthy and happy, she'd only known him for the last year of his life when he was dying. No doubt she'd have witnessed much anger and frustration over the acceptance of his illness and its indisputable outcome. I'd shared with him the best part of his life, and he the best part of mine, a time when I wasn't thought of as just someone's wife or mother, a time when I had my own identity, my own opinions, and my own independence. Our physical time together had been brief and all too long ago, but it had been precious, a unique love at a unique time in our lives.

Always at the back of my troubled mind was the regret that we never did get married and now never would. Mum helped me to view things in a different light.

'You know, marriage isn't all that special anyway,' she said. 'If you're married you often stay together because you have to. But if you don't marry, if two people stay together without that, then they're together because they want to be, not because they have to be. There's nothing holding them together except their love for each other.'

I'd never looked at it that way before. 'We were already married, anyway, weren't we?'

'Yes,' she replied. 'I suppose you were.'

'We couldn't have got married because we already were. You don't do it twice. How could we have been joined together in God's house before him when we were already joined by him?'

'That's right,' she said. 'It would never have worked, anyway. You two were so possessive of one another, one would have always been wondering where the other was, and who with.'

She was right. It had been unbearable working together, seeing each other talk and flirt with others. How much more difficult would it have proved if we hadn't worked together, with permanent thoughts of betrayal festering inside our heads?

Mum knew as I did that the main root of our problems was religion. The more we discussed the topic, the clearer it became. That the sad irony in all this was that we were joined together by God and kept apart by religion.

I still couldn't stop asking myself, why me? – especially three or four days later, when I once more found myself pacing up and down, round and round, moving from one room to the next with profoundly increased heart rate, before John's words broke the deafening silence.

The answer to everything is in Babylon! Look for it! Find it!

'What do you mean? The song or the ancient city? Which is it?'

The ancient city.

'What *is* Babylon?' I asked. 'It's significant isn't it? What does it mean?'

Absolute, complete, paradise!

'Heaven?'

Yes.

'I don't know where to start looking. What if I can't find it?'

You will. Just keep looking. It's in Babylon. Babylon holds the key to everything. Look for it. Find it. The last two instructions were repeated like a stuck record.

'All right, all right, I'll find it. Haven't got a clue what I'm supposed to be looking for, but somehow I'll find it.'

I was a bit worried. John's determination that I discover the truth was so profound I could feel every particle of it welling inside my veins. The messages wouldn't let up for a minute; he had to be sure that it came through loud and clear that it wouldn't be dismissed lightly.

Find it! Find it! he kept telling me. *Look for it and FIND IT!*

In a cold sweat I scanned the internet for any relevant information on ancient Babylon. In my desperate search, I scrolled through endless pages of information that meant little or nothing to me. Library books didn't help much either. It was like looking for a needle in a haystack, but I continued with my search.

'I can't find it, John.'

He remained insistent *Keep looking! Just keep looking and you'll find it.*

'Can't you tell me what it's all about?'

No. You've got to find out for yourself.

'OK then. I'll keep trying, but I don't know where to begin. How do I find something when I don't know what it is I'm looking for?'

Perhaps our previous existence occurred in Babylon. Maybe that's what it was all about. We always knew we'd lived before; that was all I could think of. I must be looking for two people that shared a great love together during that period of time, but with all my determined efforts, I could find nothing, at least nothing that struck any kind of recognition in me. All I'd managed to discover was that the Babylonians enjoyed writing poetry, as I did, and that they were a very advanced civilization, who had devised a 'number system' and believed everyone's life on earth was related to numbers, that numbers were the key to our whole existence.

At that point, I remembered John's message: *Babylon holds the key to everything.* That's it. It was the number system. I'd found it, but I still didn't understand its significance.

From then on, bit by bit, everything seemed slowly to fall into place, and each day I was more and more baffled and excited by my latest find. An amazing catalogue of dates and numbers linked John and me. It was truly extraordinary.

Until that point, the only thing I had ever thought a strange coincidence, apart from our sense of déjà vu, was that we shared the same zodiac sign – Sagittarius. More and more numbers would flood into my head. I discovered that John's number was three, my number was four and by adding them together, we had Mum's number, which was seven.

John was born on 30/11/63, the 30th in the year '63. I was born on 04/12/64, the 4th in the year '64. If you add up all the numbers in his date of birth it comes to 14. Mine comes to 17. The difference between the two is 3. He died on the third day of the fourth month 2001. Time of death quarter to three. Age of death 37. There were three days between John's birthday and mine.

It seemed that these three numbers were extremely significant in the lives of the three of us. We were extraordinarily linked by them, and they frequently crossed and intermingled in each of our lives. Which ever way you look or play around with any set of numbers or dates relating to John and to me, the same number patterns emerge.

We had worked together in the bingo hall surrounded by numbers. We had fallen in love with each other in an environment dominated by numbers. It was meant to happen that way, just as John had told me on our very first intimate night together.

The numbers three, four and seven are particularly religious numbers, with three being the most prominent. Anything related to the number three seems to be directly linked to God. For example:

The holy trinity.
The spirit ascends to heaven on the third day.
Jesus died aged 33.
Peter, the apostle denied knowing Jesus three times.
Jesus was betrayed for thirty pieces of silver.
There are three main church ceremonies: baptism, marriage and funeral.
The wedding ring is placed on the third finger.

Baby Jesus was visited by three wise men bearing three gifts. God is a word made up of three letters.

And if all that wasn't enough, I was later to discover that John's father was born on 30th October, the same date as mine, and died on 28th June, the same day as Robin's. The number of years between John's father's death and Robin's father's, was four! If *that* wasn't enough proof that we were all linked by numbers, one evening, when I happened to be relaxing in the bath, I decided to ask John another question. 'How long will I have to wait till I see you again?'

Reverse our dates of birth, he replied.

His birthdate, 30, becomes 03, the date of his death. Mine, 04 becomes 40. 'It comes to 40,' I told him.

That's right.

'You mean?'

You will die at 40 he said, When all the threes come together in your fortieth year. That's when. Your hair will be long. It will take all your strength.

'You're not joking, are you? I'll die at forty? There's no mistake?'

There's no mistake.

'But there's nothing wrong with me. I feel fine. I'm healthy. People who are young and healthy don't just die suddenly.'

You will!

'It won't be an accident,will it? I'd hate to die that way.'

It won't be an accident.

I began to look more closely at the numbers. If this information was correct, and my life was to end at 40, there would be three years between the year of John's death and mine, and three years between us in age of death. Mum would be 73 in my 40th year, John's age of death in reverse. The difference between 40 and 73 is 33.

I was amazed at the significance numbers had played in my life, and that I was suddenly able to make all these connections. It was a discovery I wasn't making by myself; I was being told where to look, what numbers to subtract or add to make these connections.

'Are you sure there's no mistake, John about my death at 40?'

No. You've worked it all out for yourself, through the number system.

It didn't bother me, really, knowing this; in fact I'd rather know. Death doesn't hold any fear for me, especially not now, after everything that's happened. I'm not looking forward to the actual dying process, of having to relinquish this physical body, but it's an inevitable process, one which we all have to undergo at some stage. Anyway, in all honesty, the thought of living in this world for years and years without John to share it, frightens me. It would be my idea of hell. I want to be wherever he is. We still need to be together, and although we still are, in a way, it's not as it was before. We're on opposite sides of the fence.

I'm in prison, looking out from behind the bars. I can see all the people outside, enjoying life, and I want to, but it's something that's not available to me. I try to reach out and grasp some of it for myself, but it's beyond my reach. They've all got what I want and can't have. I see death as a release from that prison. A release from the confines of my body, and from the confines of the material world.

Once you can understand what death is exactly, it becomes easier to accept. I now know death to be a living entity. It's not just something that happens to you, you don't just die. It's a living force that waits to consume the life from your physical form, drawing that life out of you like a powerful vacuum cleaner. Sucking deeper and deeper into the void. It's the pathway to the next life.

I believe that's what the dark force was, that hovered in the background when I was a child, just before my out-of-body experiences. The time of the spirit leaving the body is normally the time of death. That's why death was there, but it wasn't able to take me, because I wasn't dying. The same force had been present in my room several weeks before John's death, to forewarn me of its imminent arrival. On that occasion I experienced the suffo-cating and the discomfort that was soon to fall upon John. He was part of me after all, the other half of my own spirit. I can now say with virtual certainty, that the dark, heavy-breathing, uncomfort-able entity that gazed upon me twice in my life, was death itself, and I'm also aware with just as much certainty, that the next time I stare death in the face will be the third and final time: the time of my own death!

If you believe in God, and the resurrection, you will come out of the shadow of death, and emerge on the 'other side.' If you don't believe, you will stay shrouded in death with no hope of finding any exit.

21

Still, I kept on thinking, might there be a mistake? Perhaps I'd heard it wrong, could I be sure I'd picked up the information correctly? Each day I kept asking myself, are you sure? Is it right? Then one day, I was driving along in my car, and once again felt the need to have my question answered.

'John,' I asked one last time, 'Is this certain?'

Before anything else could be said, a huge temporary road-sign with the number 40 on it seemed to leap up at the windscreen. It was as if John was saying to me, *If you don't believe what I say, just look for yourself!* It happened at the exact instant I asked the question, and yet I hadn't even noticed the sign before that point.

Unbelievably, despite the many messages I'd received, my mind still remained doubtful, until one evening when I was pensively watching television.

All of a sudden, another voice entered my head, and this time recognition was immediate, I suddenly felt very humble and lowly, yet at the same time, honoured and privileged, as you can imagine when God himself actually speaks to you. The voice was commanding, yet warm and comforting. I immediately felt at one with this being.

John didn't lie to you. You will die at forty! Of all the voices and messages I'd received over the years, this one was the one that shook the foundations of my soul.

'Yes,' I answered obediently, with a slight nod of my head. 'What should I do? I'm married to someone that I can't love properly. All the love I have inside me is for one person. How can I cope with that?'

Follow your heart, just follow your heart! Came the reply.

'But I don't understand what you mean by that exactly. Help me to understand.'

Just follow your heart!

The voice left me. I was shocked and stunned, and to this day I still have trouble understanding the message. It was clear enough, and it makes sense to me, but what do I do? I'm all Robin has. Do I break his heart by telling him the truth? Or do I continue to live a lie? Which is right? I think of John every waking hour of the day, and most of my sleeping hours at night. I want to be with him, but can't be, not properly, not yet. How do you begin to tell someone you've been married to for nearly 18 years that you're really married to someone else and always have been? It is right that John should be with me, and God thinks so too, or else he wouldn't be with me as he is. God wouldn't have allowed it. So where does Robin fit into all this?

The following night, John and I had another of our heart-to-heart conversations.

'What's it all about, John? What's going on?'

Haven't you worked it out yet? You were special. I was too. We both were. It's all about love.

'Do you know, I have a fantasy? That one day, I would kneel down before God himself with you beside me, and that our union would be truly blessed by him.'

It already is!

'That's lovely.'

It's true. You belong to me.

'I guess we both always knew that, didn't we?' I glanced down at the band of gold glistening on my finger. *Remove it!* John instructed.

'What?'

I said remove it. It offends me.

'I can't, Robin will notice.'

Remove it!

'All right, but I'll have to put it back on later.'

I slipped the ring off my finger as requested, as I did many times after. If John asked me to remove the offending article, I always obliged just for a while. It pleased him and I liked to put him at ease.

One dull, damp day towards the end of the summer, Mum was suddenly startled by the sight of someone walking through the kitchen. The shadowy male figure wearing a black suit glided serenely past and floated out through the open back door. Although she didn't see his face, she knew it was John.

'Oh!' she screamed, 'you frightened me!'

He didn't answer.

Later she told me, 'Even though I expected to see him at some point, he still took me completely by surprise.'

Haven't people always believed in some form of after-life? Shouldn't we then ask ourselves why? Were millions of people from different cultural backgrounds and from different periods throughout history all wrong? Why do people the world over lay flowers on the graves of their departed loved ones? Because our souls know that they can and do see. Some time, someone learns the truth and tries to share that enlightenment. We can only learn if we're prepared to stop and listen, and to believe the unbelievable.

Mum and I continued with our trips to the cemetery about once a month. Each time we'd leave flowers or plants in pots or vases, only to find that they'd been removed by our next visit, but I wasn't going to let that stop me. John would often instruct me to visit the grave, and I always felt under an obligation to carry out his wishes.

His visits remained consistent. Sometimes he'd disappear for several hours or maybe even a day or two. During such times I'd still be aware of the faintest touching sensation upon me now and again, as if to let me know that although he couldn't be with me entirely, he was still with me in thought.

One night I was awakened from a deep, peaceful sleep by that easily recognizable chilled aura hovering just above my face. It was one of the most sensual experiences of my life. The love that seemed to radiate from the cold invisible vapour was truly magical. He was staring so profoundly into my sleep-filled, blurry eyes, I wanted to reach out and cuddle him, but I couldn't because he was untouchable. I absorbed all the passion and love that was being bestowed upon me, without being able to reciprocate in any way other than to smile tenderly, and try to convey my love by power of thought.

Look at the clock! he told me. It was a quarter to three. The time of his death, and the first of many times I'd be woken at that hour of the night.

'I love you,' I whispered fervently.

I love you too. Didn't say it enough before.

'It doesn't matter. You're here now.' My temperature became erratic. Cold and shivery, then indescribably hot. Subtle changes were taking place inside me like the build-up to an orgasm, creeping over me very slowly but surely, then just before the crucial moment fading away to nothing, leaving me always frustrated. It came to me that he was only permitted to go so far.

'At the end, will you be there to help me through it?' I asked nervously.

Yes.

'How will it be? What's it like to die?'

Terrible! But you reach a point when you don't really know what is happening.

I understood death to be rather like childbirth. There comes a time when the pain is unbearable, but when you reach that point, the point when you can't take it any more, the baby emerges, and it's all over. So it is with death. We're born through pain and we die through pain. It heightens the senses, makes us appreciate what comes after. You always imagine death to be an unnatural pain, unlike childbirth, but death is a natural process.

'What is the valley of the shadow of death?'

It is the closing of one door and the opening of another.

'Does it feel strange existing in your new form and your new world?'

No. Bit strange at first, but I'm used to it now.

'Will things ever be the same for us?'

Things will be better than they ever were, you've got to believe that.

'What about your former body? How do you feel about that?'

There's no emotional attachment to the body you leave behind. You are aware that it was you but that's all.

'You won't leave me again will you? I couldn't cope with you leaving again.'

No, I'll never leave.

There would be times when I'd sit and watch *Wuthering Heights* or *Ghost* with John sitting beside me, stroking me softly throughout. It was the most amazing, awe-inspiring sensation. To sit and watch those films with a ghost next to me. I'd stare with blurry, tear-filled eyes and whisper, 'But you're really dead! You're here with me like this but you're really dead!'

No, I'm not! he'd reply.

Wuthering Heights was so close to my own life, it had to have been based on personal experience. When we watched *Ghost* together, and it came to the part where the penny moves across the room, John said *I wish I could do that!* I gazed lovingly back at him, my eyes becoming fixed in the right spot, and I would blow a tender kiss. A sudden rush of air swirled back at me. He'd reciprocated. A warm pressing sensation could be felt against the side of my face. He was kissing me. He was not permitted to kiss my lips, though he could touch them with his fingers. Although he hadn't told me the rules he must abide by, some of them just seem to infiltrate my thoughts anyway.

Another restless morning would follow. That all too familiar sequence of events that would incite an important announcement. I listened to the *White Ladder* album, but could not ease my troubled state of mind.

Buy some flowers and take them to the grave today! He said.

'But I was going to take some on Tuesday. Tuesday is a much better day for me. I've got a lot on today.' Robin needed me at work that morning, and for the afternoon we'd made arrangements to take the girls out.

I know you're busy, but please do this for me. It must be today! Not Tuesday, today!

I knew I couldn't let him down, but it meant my schedule was now even more hectic than before. To pick up Mum, buy the flowers and take them to the cemetery without Robin finding out, and all within a limited amount of time, so I could be at work when he needed me, and finished in time for the outing, was a task and a half. How would I cram it all in? I remained perplexed over the sudden change in plan.

'Come on John, what's it all about?'

I need to know that you'll put me first, and do this for me.

I arrived at Mum's in my usual state of agitation.

'We've got to visit the cemetery now!' I told her.

'Why? What's going on? What's the rush? I'm not ready. I'll have to change.'

'Never mind that. Just get into the car. I don't really know what it's all about, maybe you can ask him later for me, when things have settled down.'

I ran like a lunatic, charging around at full speed in order to get everything together, and much to my relief, I managed it without Robin being any the wiser. I bought the flowers, took them to the grave, and placed them on top, just as I'd been instructed to do.

As I climbed back into the car, Mum said that John had spoken to her. *Tell Amanda thanks for coming today. I knew she would.*

Before the day was over, Mum phoned me to say she'd had a second conversation with our mutual friend. As usual, she relayed the message word for word.

I knew that if Amanda could do this one thing for me because I asked her to, on a day when she was so busy, then I would finally know that she put me first, above everything else.

180

'John, you've always known that Amanda puts you first.'

Yes, but I never really believed it.

This confirmed what he'd told me earlier in the day, and that night when I went to sleep, he gave me a sort of 'present' as a thank you for what I'd done.

We'd spoken many times over the past few months about the fact that we'd never had children together. He would have made a good father, and I think I might have been a better mother. A little part of both of us growing inside me as testament to our love, would have been a unique feeling of joyous ecstasy. We'd never known that joy. 'We should have had a child together,' I told him. 'Now I'll never know what that would have felt like.'

Little did I know that this experience was not lost to me completely, and that as I drifted into sleep, a strange dream would carry me into an alternative world. In the first part of the dream, I was sitting in my old chair in Mum's house, my substantially enlarged stomach protruded in front of me, and there was considerable movement coming from inside it.

'What's happening?' I shouted. 'What's happening to me?' I was still well aware that in real life I wasn't pregnant.

The voice that answered me was John's.

You wanted to know what it would have felt like!

Then the dream changed. I was now on the telephone to John. I could see him clearly, and his voice was exactly as I remembered. He was in hospital, sitting on the bed and wearing a dressing gown. I told him that I would come and visit, and he said that would be nice. He'd like to see me. He looked forward to seeing me. This had been something else I'd discussed with John, my regret over not visiting him in hospital when he was dying; my guilt over not being there when he needed me. It was as if he was showing me what he knew I wanted to see.

When I woke the next morning I felt remarkably happy. It had been wonderful to hear John's voice again after so long and to see his face again, if only in a dream. John had put these images inside my head to ease my troubled conscience. It was a precious gift, and one I' d remember always.

My next dream however, would surpass anything I'd ever known before. It wasn't a 'normal' dream. I knew it at the time, and when I woke up. I had actually got up that morning, made breakfast, seen the kids off to school, then returned to bed for half an hour. I dozed off, not into a deep sleep, but I wasn't really awake either; sort of in between the two. (During this state, the mind seems to be most receptive to messages and images from the spirit world). I was lying on the bed in my old room at Mum's house again, only my feet were where my head should have been. I was staring at the window. John's spirit began to rise slowly upwards, as it had that day in my living room. The other side of the window was open, and in drifted a white dove. It glided through the air serenely, as it came towards me, but before it touched me, it began to glide backwards, out through the open window. Next, my vision disappeared and I heard that familiar ringing in my ears that precedes an out-of-body experience. I knew what to expect next, but it didn't happen. There seemed to be an invisible hand pushing me back, telling me I couldn't leave my body because it wasn't time. I woke up with a jolt. I had no idea at the time that the holy spirit is said to come in the form of a white dove, yet the meaning of the dream was crystal clear to me. When the time was right I would follow the holy spirit just as John had done, but not yet. I had to wait.

This was followed by a second unusual dream. I found myself in outer space; stars were all around me against a backdrop of inky black sky. There was a wise old man sitting in a chair in front of me; he was about to tell me the meaning of life. At that moment Robin woke me. But I was left in no doubt about one thing, that the answers to many of life's questions lay up there in the universe beyond our skies. Sometimes things just seem to come to me, and I'm not exactly sure why they do. It was something that never happened before John's death. I think he tries to tell me things, but there are some things he can't tell me in detail; he can only give me clues. The rest I have to discover myself. What purpose do all those planets serve? Why is it that we're led to believe that heaven is up there in the sky? Is that where the dead go, to other planets? And who or what is God? The ancient Egyptians worshipped the sun, and spent much time studying and observing the stars and their position in the night sky. They also believed the answers to be up there, high above us.

'I believe God is the sun,' Mum has told me many times. 'When I was a child in school, whenever the sun shone on me, I always felt closer to God.' Something tells me she's not wrong. Jesus said he was the light of the world. The most powerful force in our world and the greatest source of light is the sun itself. It is born at daybreak, it rises, at dusk it expires. The following day it will rise again. We follow this sequence of events. We are born, we flourish and die. We come again. We can't gaze into it because it hurts our eyes, yet people who have had near-death experiences tell us of a brilliant light at the end of a dark tunnel that doesn't hurt the eyes. Is the dark tunnel a voyage through space? It's time we thought hard about that.

John had the power to let me see beyond the visible. With each new day, things became clearer and clearer. Answers poured into my brain. This is what I was told. God is a 'diverse and complex energy'. For anything to become whole it needs an opposite, ie; light/dark, hot/cold. One complements the other. When we are cold we need heat, when in the dark we need light. We cannot know what is good without knowing what is evil. The energy is there to be used in whichever way we choose. God is positive energy. Satan controls the negative side but it comes from the same source.

There is no such thing as death for those who believe. Death is rebirth, the rebirth of a purer, wiser version of the former self. When you pass through the tunnel, you leave the bad behind. That's what dies: all the bad things about yourself, the anger and the bitterness.

The purpose of life on earth is to learn about yourself, about the real you, and about the influences your actions have on other people and their lives. The three most important things are love, forgiveness and knowledge. If you can do these three things well, then you are truly close to God. This life is for making mistakes, and learning from them. This is the life where we are allowed to make mistakes. The next will be better because we will have developed our knowledge about ourselves. We are taught that Jesus is the resurrection and the life, and those who believe in him will never die. What this means in simple terms is that whoever believes that Jesus was crucified, and rose again on the third day, will have eternal life through that belief in him, will be born again in his image, we will take on his form.

Those who fail to learn about God or about themselves in this lifetime, or refuse to accept the truth, have to come back again, hence reincarnation. Once you've gained enough knowledge, and have accepted the truth, you will then go on to eternal paradise after death.

Life is just a learning process. There will be a judgement day, but not in order to be punished by God. You, yourself are the assessor of your own actions, and that day is for each of us to realize what kind of people we have been and to shame us into being better individuals.

True happiness comes from love, not from material possessions. In the end, love is all there is. God is the only truth, and the door to eternal life, but we ourselves hold the key.

There *is* only one God and one religion, something that many people fail to see. We just choose to interpret this one religion in many different ways. The important issues are the same in every religion.

Jesus came into the world to give sight to those who could not see, and to take it away from some who could; to enlighten those who are confused about the truth, those who want to believe, but need guidance. Those who are too stubborn and arrogant to open their hearts to the truth, those not willing to learn, should remain blinded by their ignorance.

That is the purpose of this book, I'm told; to enlighten those who yearn for further knowledge, not to coerce those who remain bigoted. Satan's strongest weapon against God is to make people believe that there is no God.

True love always meets with many obstacles. People try to get in the way and destroy what's good, try to destroy the indestructible. Yet to see examples of the power of love, we only have to look at disasters such as the collapse of the World Trade Center, an act of pure wickedness and terrorism, yet the public outpouring of love, compassion and unity, overshadowed this evil. Acts of terror generate love. What does this tell us?

I had always wondered how it was possible to forgive such wickedness. How can we forgive those who murder and rape? The answer is, by accepting that these people aren't truly in control of their actions. Satan attacks the weak-minded. He commits these depraved acts, using human beings as weapons to carry out his wishes. Such people often say they heard voices telling them to do what they did. These people aren't mad, and they're not stupid either, just too weak to keep him out. They allow him to take over their minds. I have heard these voices too throughout my life, just as I have heard the good ones. I have never heard them telling me to do anything wicked, just trying to turn a good thought or memory into a bad one. You have to be strong-willed to keep them from polluting your mind. A way forward can only be achieved by peaceful methods. If we allow ourselves to feel anger and bitterness and hatred towards people, we're allowing Satan to manipulate us, too. We're allowing a wicked thought to override a good one. That is why we must learn to forgive in our search for the truth. It's one of the hardest things to learn, but it is possible.

John has been able to forgive me for marrying and having children with someone else. I have been able to forgive him. Whatever he did or didn't do, wasn't it mostly due to me, in the end? My selfish actions caused a chain reaction of pain across many lives, not just mine and John's. How many people suffered for what I did? I have had to think hard about who I am.

22

There was still something more that John needed to tell me. It troubled him greatly, that much I knew from the intensity of pressure that had started to build inside my head one evening, an overwhelming, frustrating head-exploding pressure.

I'm not the person you think I am, he said. *I felt anger and pain for what you did but couldn't hate you. I was angry and hurt, had been drinking. I took it out on other women. I abused women. Systematic abuse of women.*

'I still love you' I told him. 'Everyone has a darker side.'

And I'm yours, he answered, sparking anxiety and fear in me.

Mum informed me he'd been making appearances at her house. His restless state of mind seemed to precipitate manifestations on a daily basis, but of only half his image, she'd tell me.

'What do you mean, half?' I asked

'He only has half a face. The other side isn't there. He's incomplete.'

We were one spirit divided into two halves before birth, a male half and a female half, but each, half of the same person. He needed me for completion. We couldn't marry in this life because marriage only lasts 'as long as you both shall live.' Our marriage was never going to end with death; our marriage and our love was immortal. This life has been like a holiday for us, some time away to realize just how much the other really means.

Those who are joined together other than as God's word doth allow, are not joined together by him, neither is their matrimony lawful. I was and still am joined to only one person, the person

186

whom God himself chose for me. How could I be married to Robin, when I was already married to John? The vows I took in St John's church on my wedding day, were they even valid?

All those messages that never made any sense to me throughout my life have now become clear. I see now why on all those unhappy nights I was told, *one day you'll be writing it down*. I smiled in disbelief over such crazy thoughts, but they were not my own. This was my purpose in life, to give information. As Satan uses people to cause harm and destruction, so God has used me to convey wisdom and understanding. 'Why me?' I've asked myself a thousand times. There are so many people better equipped educationally than me. All I can think of is that I have experienced a very rare kind of love. Being highly-educated is one thing, but to describe this type of love, one has to live it, and perhaps the fact that I don't use complicated words means that what I have to say will be more easily understood.

Our next cemetery visit would see me take a potted plant instead of the usual bunch of flowers, a yellow bush rose. *Buy that one!* John had instructed. *I like the yellow one!*

So be it, then. I took it to his graveside and placed it firmly in the centre. Several times during the course of the month I returned to water it, but on my fourth visit I noticed that a distinct change had taken place. The buttery yellow roses had turned pink.

'Don't be ridiculous,' said Mum, when I told her. I took her to see for herself; she was as speechless as I had been.

When it began to die off I decided to dig it up and replace it; Mum kept it in her back garden for me. That night she decided to rearrange some silk flowers by splitting them into separate vases. When she got up next day, John told her to go and take a look at them. The stems of the cream flowers had developed pink buds on them. These were artificial flowers yet just like the rose they'd turned pink. She showed them to me on my next visit and I just stared disbelievingly.

Meanwhile despite Mum's best attempts to revive the rose it

was fading fast, until one day John told her to go outside and inspect it. *Go and look* he said. *There are three new buds. One for me and Amanda and one for you.* Sure enough there were three new buds, yellow once again.

Why have you got the rose? he asked her.

'Amanda left it here.'

Amanda bought that rose for me. She should have it. It's been the closest thing to my previous body form. She planted it on my grave and I turned it pink. Give Amanda the rose!

'He wants you to have it,' she told me, so I took it home and placed it in a sheltered spot. It is still alive and bloomed again this summer. Some flowers were yellow; some started off yellow then turned pink.

John was undergoing subtle changes. Death seems to have different stages. As well as my face and hair, he had now also acquired the ability to touch other parts of my body too. Arms, legs, feet, hands, chest, back, stomach and intimate areas. The sensation was like rippling water moving over my skin. There were times when I could feel the bedclothes move by themselves very gently over my legs, as though he were in bed with me, and one day he'd been tickling my face when I laughed in such a way that my mouth fell open. As I took in some air, I seemed to take him in also. There were special moments when he'd let me touch him with my fingertip. It was like touching moving hair.

Meanwhile Mum told me that John's presence at her house was becoming almost constant. 'He's here all the time,' she told me, 'but only half here. When you come you seem to bring the other half of him with you and then he's complete. It sounds silly but that's how it is.' It wasn't silly to me. When John left a room he took part of me with him.

There would be days when I'd feel his touch upon me but was unable to see him, whereas Mum could. She'd tell me that he was kneeling down at my feet by the chair, a position he frequently took up. My arm or face would be stroked tenderly or my toes would be kissed.

'He sits in your chair, when you're not here, waiting for you. When you are here, he sits on the floor. He says he's used to sitting on the floor, so he doesn't mind.'

'That's right' I told her. 'He often sat on the floor, both here, and at his family home. There were always so many people in their house, there never seemed to be enough seats for everyone. John often ended up sitting on the floor. I thought Dad usually sits in this chair, when I'm not here?' I added.

'Well, he doesn't now. He says it always seems to be reserved.'

'What is it exactly that you see, when you say you can see John?'

'I see a grey-outlined mummified image.'

'I wish I could see him,' I replied looking downwards to the space where my hand had just slipped momentarily from the arm of the chair, and was now being tenderly stroked. I smiled. He was smiling back at me, but I couldn't see, only sense it.

After one such day spent like this, I announced it was time to go home and get the tea ready, and I beckoned John to follow me.

'Come on,' I said, 'we're leaving now.'

'My God,' said Mum, 'I don't believe it. He's been sitting beside you the whole time, but now he's standing. He's stood up, and now he's walking towards you.'

'Well, he wasn't going to walk out on his knees was he?' I replied flippantly.

'He's coming with you.'

'Of course he is. He does what I ask. I do what he asks. That's how it is.'

I have discovered that John has three ways of appearing: white, as in the vapourized image, grey, the mummified outline and black, the shadowy image of his former self. I am told this is because death has three phases: rebirth, development and ascension. As the physical body decomposes, the spiritual body becomes a more 'complete entity'.

Our relationship has three stages. The first was when we were both physical. The second is now, where I'm still physical, and he's spiritual. The third and final stage, will be when we are both spiritual. I'm all too aware that I mustn't see him until the specifically designated time, so I'm glad he has persistently allowed Mum to see him.

One evening, just after I'd made myself some dinner, and taken it into the living room to eat it on my knee. I saw what I can only describe as the shadow of a man's shoes walking towards me, on top of the shadow that my sofa was making on the carpet. Three steps came towards me from nowhere, then disappeared. As I began to wonder if I'd just seen what I thought I'd seen, John stroked my face and I felt the breeze. *You did just see me!* John confirmed.

In the next three days, on several separate occasions, I thought I saw someone dart with great velocity from one room in the house to another. It had to be John. I'd watched him flit around so many times at work, I knew his type of movement. He seemed to be doing his utmost to let me know he was still very much alive and with me. Then he'd disappear for several days, not entirely gone, but not entirely present either.

Following a short period of absence from Mum's he made a dramatic comeback one day in the form of a butterfly, which landed on her knee as she sat in the garden.

Hi, said John, as the tiny creature landed.

'Where have you been?' Mum asked. 'You haven't been here for a few days.'

I've had things to do. Came the reply.

'Amanda thought you'd forsaken her.'

I have not, came a most assertive answer.

I arrived a little later. Marched through to the rear garden and sat myself down on the bench. John began to stroke my arm.

'Do you see that bush over there?' Mum said pointing along the fence. 'John told me I'm to cut one of the roses for you.'

'That's nice,' I replied. But the thought passed away until it was time for me to leave. Just before waving me on my way John promptly jogged her memory.

'He's just reminded me' she said. 'I'm to give you a rose.' She ran back outside to cut one. I could almost see his love filled eyes as she handed it to me. I smiled. 'From beyond the grave,' she said, placing it between my fingers.

'Thanks John,' I whispered. The coldness swirled and his fingers swept tenderly across my cheek. For all the heartache I'd suffered throughout my turbulent past, I'd had so many to precious moments to compensate.

One evening later that week. Mum remembered that she'd left her doormat outside to dry, opened the front door and bent down in the glow from the setting sun to retrieve it, and was suddenly aware of a man's black shoes set firmly on the ground in front of her. She assumed it was her insurance man, who often called at that time of day, and raised her head until she reached his waist level – at that moment the phantasm passed straight through her body like a gust of wind. She was left shaken and bewildered. I was anxious to know how it felt.

'What's it like? What did you feel? Was it a shivery sensation?'

'No,' she replied. 'It was weird. I felt his legs go through my legs, and I was left temporarily stunned. I couldn't move. It was a very, very strange sensation. I didn't see his face.'

I made notes for the book. A tremendous surge of cold air swept up behind me and I knew he was looking over my shoulder to see what I'd written. I must admit I was a little nervous at first, as I anticipated a sarcastic comment, but he kept quiet. He observed, and he read my words in silence. He's never discussed the book with me, oddly enough, except to ask me occasionally how it's coming along. I've told him repeatedly that whatever I include must be with his full agreement, I've made that quite clear from the start. He's never commented. He'll often sit with me while I'm typing away. He's with me now. Sometimes I ask for help in remembering. He doesn't answer, but some of my memories become more vivid afterwards, or I recall things that I'd previously forgotten. When I worked on the religious pages, it felt as if I was typing words that someone else was dictating. The writing of this book has been more arduous than I believed possible. I need time to do it properly, yet time is the one thing that I don't have. I am watched continuously. I can't work at night because everyone is at home. By day Robin phones me continually, but I rarely hear the telephone. This prompts him to ask what I've been doing all day, every day. He thinks I have a lover. He visits home at various different times throughout the day. As soon as I hear his van pull up outside, I make a frantic attempt to remove any evidence from the computer, and clear away my papers. I can't do anything when the girls are home from school, and when Robin returns home from work he wants a detailed account on how I've spent my time. I've become an expert at whizzing round the house in half an hour, trying to make it look as if I've been hard at it for the best part of the day. I'd love to tell him that I've spent seven hours on the computer, then cut the grass, hoovered the house, dusted, prepared tea, and my eyes can hardly focus, but it's easier for him to think that I've just been lazy.

I have a computer at work I can use too though I still encounter the same problems. Each time the door opens I think it's Robin, returned unexpectedly, and I shake with fear and hurriedly clear my work from the desk. I've had one or two close shaves. I sneak papers in and out of the house keeping them under lock and key. All my hopes and prayers are that they remain undisturbed. Whenever I feel the need to write something down, and the family are at home, it becomes a meticulously-planned exercise. Scribbled notes on pieces of paper have to be hidden in various places until the next day, when they can be safely added to the others. My younger daughter constantly crashes into my room to ask, 'What are you doing, Mum?' Or Robin appears, to ask what I'm reading and why. I have a book beside me as a decoy, and say, that I'm engrossed in some great love story; which of course I am. I find myself under surveillance all day long until I switch off my bedside light and go to sleep. Even then, I wonder Robin hasn't rigged up some technical device to monitor my dreams. Trying to make a good job of something under these conditions is virtually impossible. I feel like a criminal in my own home.

On top of everything else, I experience little sparks of light at various different points in the room, usually when sitting quietly watching TV, or sometimes when working in the kitchen. They're not continuous. I might just see one or two over a period of several days. It's made me think about the saying 'seeing the light'. Perhaps the more spiritual knowledge you gain, the more of God's light you are able to see.

In sharp contrast, however, I have often seen dark shadows moving at speed just outside my field of vision. I wonder if it's John's attempt at letting me know he's in the room with me. Mum has seen them too.

John remains as crude and sarcastic as he ever was. One night while relaxing with a cup of tea I suddenly got, *Why are you wearing a blanket for a skirt?* I laughed out loud to that remark, and needless to say I've been reluctant to wear the grey tweed garment since. He called me 'panda eyes' when I tried out a new eye-shadow. When Mum mentioned one day that she'd been preparing fish for tea, and her hands still smelled fishy, *Isn't that just like a woman?* John interrupted. Again when I pulled a new black-and-cream underwear set from the bag to ask Mum what she thought of it he chirped in, *Very sexy!*

Robin made plans for us to celebrate his 40th birthday in Prague. John told Mum he was absolutely *bloody pissed off* because I was leaving him behind. He came with me anyway. I was a little worried at the thought of spending several days alone with Robin; I knew he viewed this as a golden opportunity for a romantic weekend together, but that was the last thing on my mind.

We spent the first night in a hotel at Heathrow airport. As we prepared for bed, Robin switched on the television, and to my delight David Gray was singing 'Babylon'. It seemed too far fetched to be true, just as on my first trip away after John's death, when David Gray seemed to be following me. The only way this could be possible was if everything in life was already pre-determined, and when events coincide it isn't just coincidental. It happens because it was always going to. You meet someone at a predestined time because that's how it's meant to be. John wasn't making these things happen, as I'd first thought, they were happening because circumstances were prearranged to make such coincidences occur.

After we'd put the lights out, John's presence became even stronger. He began to caress me lovingly all over, very gentle, yet determined. He swept mysteriously over my entire body, first my nose and the left side of my face, then arms, stomach, toes and lastly between my legs. There was warm pressure on the side of my face as he kissed, and cold, sensual breezes that drove me into a frenzy of sexual passion. Robin was fast asleep, and knew nothing of my pleasurable encounter. I was aching for John, now more than ever; my soul was alive and dancing, my body aroused, and my eyes captivated. Once more I asked myself, 'How can I be feeling so wonderful?' The last time I'd felt so happy was the last time John and I shared a similar intimate moment. The closer he gets, the closer I want him to be, and the harder it gets for us to become any closer. It's an impossible situation. He takes me to the very brink of ecstasy, then holds me back, because what comes next is strictly for the after-life. How do I finish what he has started? I've found a way that I believe to be mutually enjoyable, and for now we have to make that do. He's permitted to take part in intimate activities with me, of a kind, as long as he remains aware of the boundaries.

Next day, I felt tired, not surprisingly, and I yawned throughout breakfast.

That's what you get for playing with yourself all night.

I giggled into my tea cup. 'Well, you started it.'

And you finished it!

My eyes sped around the room. I knew that no one else could hear his crass comments, but I blushed all the same.

'What are you smiling at?' Robin asked, very suspicious.

The loving touches continued throughout the flight. I seemed to sense that John was sitting in the aisle next to my seat. The entire break in Prague was spent with him following me, touching me and loving me in much the same way he did at home, tickling me either on or inside the nose, and always causing me to react in a suspicious way. My lips would tingle and vibrate. I could feel my hair being gently ruffled; if I were to look in a mirror afterwards it would be visibly messed up. Sometimes I'd be caught in the middle, with Robin touching me on one side, and John endeavouring to outdo him on the other. At no time was I ever in any doubt as to what was happening or who was instigating these pleasurable episodes. So many different things occurred that were definitely *not* an imaginary series of events.

Robin's 40th birthday passed by without any sexual advances from me. How could I make any? John's presence had been so overwhelming. But Robin had sensed something amiss. Once or twice he caught me as I smiled adoringly into space, or winked when there was no one to wink at. He'd ask me what was going on. 'Nothing' I'd reply unconvincingly.

'You're lying.' He was right. I was a lousy liar. This was strange territory for me. All my life I'd prided myself on being truthful. Telling lies didn't come naturally to me, and it's not something I felt comfortable with. I had no choice but to lie. How could I even begin to explain what was happening to me? I'd always told Robin everything, and I wanted to tell him this now. In 17 years of marriage we'd never had any secrets from each other, except my true feelings for John.

I've tried many times to suggest the truth in a roundabout sort of way, but he's not prepared to listen. I once made a futile attempt at telling him I had proof of life after death, that if I'd been wrong about every single thing in my life up to that point, I wasn't wrong about this. He just called me a religious maniac and said I was talking rubbish. *Let the blind remain blind,* a voice tells me, *he doesn't deserve to know.*

On my first visit to Mum's following the Prague trip I had begun to tell her all about it when all of a sudden her face turned ashen, her mouth fell open, and she stared into space with a fuddled expression.

'What is it? What's wrong?' I asked.

'I don't believe it. John's just entered the room. Floated over the top of the table and now he's sitting in your chair. It's unbelievable, he hasn't been here since before you went away. You were right, you must have brought him back with you.'

I was dying to turn around and take a look, but I knew I couldn't. 'I told you he's been with me, and I've felt him with me all morning. I just can't see him because it's not allowed. Now that I'm back I want to visit the grave and take some flowers.'

'We'll go together,' she replied, 'and that will do then until his birthday.' She suddenly spat out her tea and began to choke with laughter.

'What's wrong with you now?' I asked.

'He's just said,' she could hardly utter the words, 'he's just said … *That's bloody weeks away!*'

The easiest way for me to cope with my loss, apart from reliving memories and talking them through with Mum, was to take flowers to the cemetery on a regular basis. The planning of each floral tribute, no matter how small, was something that meant a great deal to me. I needed to show John just how important he was, and still is in my life, and this was all I could do. I couldn't show him in any other way. I began to make preparations for his impending birthday and also a little further ahead, for Christmas.

The short course in flower arranging I'd taken some years before, was now proving invaluable. I bought some florist's foam and constructed an elaborate spray of mixed flowers in white, burgundy and yellow, against a backdrop of green ivy and other assorted foliage. Mum made a smaller spray arrangement.

We took the flowers to the grave the day before the 30th, as we thought it too risky to go on the day itself. Forty-eight hours later I returned to see what else had been left. Karen's spray of red and purple carnations took centre stage, someone had left three flowers tied together with some ribbon around them in West Ham colours, and there was a small bunch of flowers with the wrapping still on from his mother. I was greatly relieved to discover that my flowers had been left in place. Mum's had disappeared.

There were various tributes in the evening paper that night. One from the family, one from Karen, and one from David. I had decided not to put anything in.

On our next visit a couple of weeks later, I was overcome by an urge to look for his father's grave, but I had no idea where to look. There were hundreds of headstones. All I had to go on was that John and his father shared the same name.

I parked the car at random, and began my walk along the first row, peering at the names along the way. I was only about halfway along when I saw it – just a plain wooden cross like John's, no age, no date of death, just a name, completely overgrown with weeds. Someone had visited at sometime in the past, as there were the remnants of what had once been flowers. It was one of the worst graves in the entire cemetery.

Suddenly, I saw what John's might look like in a few years' time, with the same name on the same humble cross. It was eerie, and extremely sad.

'John must have told you where to look,' said Mum. 'There are so many graves here, and yet you found it so easily.'

'You know John's will probably go the same way? I expected to see a headstone by now.'

Nothing would have made me happier than to see his resting-place well cared for and full of flowers, but sadly it *was* already beginning to go the way of his father's.

23

The day after John's birthday Mum had some trouble with her smoke alarm. It would wake her up in the early hours of the morning with its excruciating 'beeping' noise, going on and off for no apparent reason. Eventually, she lost patience and removed the batteries. Remarkably, the ear-piercing noise persisted. This was a ridiculous situation, so she hurled the offending article into the outside dustbin where, despite being without batteries, it relentlessly continued to 'beep'.

The next day she went into town to buy a new one. As soon as she got it home and fixed it to the ceiling it began to 'beep'. It continued to sound on and off over the days leading up to my birthday, when it miraculously stopped.

'What the hell is going on, John?' she asked, well aware it was someone's idea of a joke. 'This noise is driving me mad.'

Ask Beeper. This had been John's pet name for me. I was highly amused when she told me. Was there a point he was trying to make? Anyway the past was the past, and today was my birthday. John was with me, and we both set off by car for a day's shopping in Peterborough.

Robin had made plans for us to spend New Year at a hotel by the seaside. There would be a formal gala dinner and other social gatherings which required the appropriate attire. I was in urgent need of an evening dress. As I moved from shop to shop, and picked out some possibles, John would butt in *I don't like that one. That's horrible!* or, *that's nice. I like that.*

As I made my way through the shopping centre, John's presence alongside me became more pronounced. I knew he was leering at me. Staring at my chest then into my face just like he used to do, trying his best to make me laugh. I fought to keep a solemn expression, but from time to time, I could only grin and blush.

'Will you stop making me laugh?' I insisted. 'People will think I'm mad.'

You are.

'Seriously, everyone's staring at me, like I'm some sort of a nutter.'

They'd be right.

I continued to wink at him, just to let him know I was still aware of his ever-increasing aura. Then it occurred to me that some stranger might think I was winking at them, and get the wrong idea. My eyes drifted through the crowds, and an endless sea of faces. I wondered then, as I do now, is there anyone else out there among all those hundreds of different people who experiences the same things that I do, or is it just me?

That night my daughter Kimberley ran into the kitchen with a very important announcement. 'Mum, I swear this house is haunted! You won't believe this – I saw a figure at the bottom of the stairs.'

'I believe you,' I responded .

'No joke' she continued. 'It was really spooky.'

Robin entered the room. 'What are you talking about?' He asked.

'Kimberley saw a ghost in the hall.'

'Don't talk such crap.'

Let the blind remain blind, I thought.

The following night she saw him again. I'd been sitting comfortably in my rocking chair listening to the *White Ladder* album, when I left the room momentarily to fetch something. During my absence Kimberley entered, and was startled by the ghostly figure of a man as he walked from the rocking chair towards the CD player.

'Mum, I've seen it again! I really have. It was in the dining room!'

'Don't worry about it. It's all right. Nothing to be worried about.' I answered reassuringly. I so wanted to tell her that she hadn't imagined it, but once again I had to conceal the truth.

The fact that he'd allowed someone else to witness his presence only strengthened Mum's and my belief. Kimberley knew nothing of my relationship with John. Three of us could not have been mistaken; in fact four, for my seven-year-old niece had also experienced some strange occurrences while staying with Mum. She'd been lying upstairs one day on the bed in my old room when she suddenly came running downstairs.

'Nanny, is there someone else here with us?' she asked worriedly.

'No, Florence, just you and me. Why?'

'I just thought I saw something. And Nanny, what's a nightmare?'

'It's a horrible scary dream.'

'But to dream you have to be asleep. I wasn't asleep, and these eyes were just staring at me, just staring.'

Mum told her she'd probably imagined it, but had she?

Christmas was nearing fast and I had to think about my next floral display for the grave. I'd been musing for weeks over various different options, and how I would manage to transport the finished article at the appropriate time. Once the schools had broken up it would prove difficult, so it had to be done before then, though if too soon, the flowers would be past their best by Christmas Day.

I decided on a wreath in West Ham colours, so I made my way to Mum's house equipped with plenty of greenery from my garden, including some cuttings from a very pretty evergreen shrub with delicate white flowers, some stunning burgundy roses, and two ribbons, one pale blue, and one burgundy edged with gold.

I wrapped up well as it was quite cold and set to work in the back garden. Mum made some tea while I spent the following hour and a half putting it all together. John watched me studiously throughout. Every so often he would brush the side of my nose or cheek very gently. It was strange that I could feel him despite the severity of the December gusts. Whenever I ventured indoors for a warm-up, he followed.

I was determined to make a good job, and after inserting some gold fircones I was quite pleased with the result. The roses were my centrepiece, flanked by the little white flowers and festooned by the bowed ribbons. The only thing that I remained unsure of was my positioning of the roses, which looked a little odd to my unskilled eye, until Mum pointed out they formed a perfect heart shape. I hadn't planned it that way, but the roses did form a heart; it was quite amazing.

All that remained now was for us to carry it from the rear garden through the house, and into the waiting car.

In trying to be helpful, Mum lifted my wreath and began transportation down the hall. She has a very tiny porch, and as she squeezed around the corner, she caught my display on some dried flowers. The two wrestled for a few seconds, and Mum's arthritic, and increasingly nervous fingers grappled with each, as she made a desperately unsuccessful attempt at holding on. My pride and joy was flung inadvertently into the air, and landed with a great thud upside down on the porch floor. The vase that had precipitated the disturbance, followed simultaneously, creating a carpet of crushed twigs, desiccated leaves and flower heads.

'What the hell have you done to my flowers?' I screamed.

'I don't believe this!' Mum yelled back.

'YOU don't believe it! All my hard work!'

We couldn't help but laugh. In an area the size of a large cardboard box, we struggled to clear the mess. The door half open, the vase rolling around on the floor, leftover dried flowers everywhere, and my my poor wreath flat on its face in the middle.

'And don't you bloody laugh,' I said as I turned around in acknowledgement of John's ever profound attendance. The look on his face in my mind's eye, only boosted my giggling.

Mum turned the wreath the right way up, and to our surprise it was still intact. One or two small pieces of greenery needed adjusting, but everything else was still remarkably in place.

'Lucky for you,' I told Mum.

'I'm really sorry' she replied.

'It's all right, no harm done thankfully.'

We went on to the cemetery, and left the flowers in place. I hoped they would look OK for Christmas; indeed I hoped they would still be there for Christmas. It would be January before we could go and check, when the kids were safely back at school, and Robin safely back at work.

That year it wasn't the kids that woke me up early on Christmas morning, but John.

Get your knickers off then – I want to give you one.

'I beg your pardon? What did you say to me?'

You heard. Get them off. Happy Christmas.

What followed next made me blush all over; every inch of me was caressed with loving care and attention. It was magical. In my wildest dreams I could never have imagined this was how things would one day turn out between us.

It feels very strange for me to have John existing in the world that we both talked of so many times. He's crossed that border, and now knows everything there is to know, while I remain still relatively in the dark. I've tried many times to extract more information about his new environment, but for all my probing, all I have managed to gather are shreds of information. 'You'll never tell me will you, not even for the book?' No answer. 'It must be lovely to watch every sunrise and sunset with the person you love. Are there sunsets where you are?'

Beautiful sunsets.

'Must be a beautiful place. I wish I was there with you now.'

It is. I wish you were here too.

Christmas came and went. New Year was looming and Robin and I made preparations for our seaside trip. I began to feel unwell. Robin was soon to follow. What began as a vague feeling of malaise turned into several weeks of uncontrollable shivering, endless trips to the toilet and a final diagnosis of food poisoning. I'd never felt so ill in my life. The trip was cancelled, and the entire vile episode reached its peak on New Year's Eve when I contracted viral meningitis. The doctor had already started us off on a course of antibiotics, but that night I just got worse and worse. Sweat poured from my body, my face resembled a boiled lobster, and the pain in my head was indescribable. It was impossible to move even the slightest fraction without feeling as if someone was smashing it hard into a brick wall. Light of any description seared into my eyes like a laser. I felt I was dying. A red rash crept down one side of my face and it began to feel puffy and swollen. John stroked it with much tenderness and caring. He tried hard to make me feel better.

'John, why can't I just die now and be with you?'

Because your work isn't done yet.

'I know,' I replied. 'I wish it was. I feel awful.'

Try to rest, you'll feel better tomorrow.

The fact that John stayed with me dutifully throughout my worst moments lifted my spirits enormously. After all, that's what love is, caring for someone when they need you most. It hit home hard yet again that when John needed me most, I was somewhere else.

Depression always seems more pronounced throughout January than any other month, I find. After such a horrific start to the year my melancholic mood seemed to deepen. I huddled by the fire on endless dark nights, spent afternoons staring into a barren landscape of inanimate stick trees under grey, heavy snow-filled skies. Warmly-clothed, I took lonely walks across the ice, thinking how sad and empty were the many winters I've walked alone without his smile to warm me, without his words of comfort, his love-filled eyes to fire the winter chill.

Winter Daydream

January frost and cold winds blow,
Lengthy nights intensify,
Snowflakes fog the window pane
As thoughts of you go drifting by.
Time has drawn a curtain
Around those happy years,
Pictures, words, just memories
Clouded by the tears.
Hold my love close to your own
As I have always done,
Keep warm our hearts together,
Till they may beat as one.

Spring awakening

When dawn smiles down with tenderness
And wakes a sleepy day,
Your kiss will wake my senses,
And steal my breath away.
When burnished golden sun unfurls,
And birdsong fills the sky,
Dawn chorus rouse my dormant heart,
And send my spirit high.
When shadows leave a dimming world
As sun begins to fade,
Take hold my hand, return my soul
To that perfect world we made.

24

With my recovery came an overwhelming urge to return to the cemetery. John had willingly played his part, now I must play mine.

It had been cold, wet and miserable. I knew my display would be well past its best, so I bought some fresh flowers. My wreath was still there, and although that pleased me, I was saddened to see that Mums had been removed yet again. My feet squelched in the river of water that had developed around his resting place. As I dug my container in, filthy water bubbled up. I hated to think of his precious body lying in that waterlogged clay soil. I secured my pot in the centre, and filled it with the replacement flowers, leaving the wreath in place as it still looked presentable. The grave was crying out for some love and attention. At least it looked a little brighter once I'd finished.

The next big occasion would be Valentine's Day, our special day. It had been a long time since I'd thought about valentines, and it was still a long way off, but I needed to plan ahead. Whatever I decided on must be fitting and professional. It didn't cross my mind to have an arrangement constructed by a florist. Good or bad, it had to be by my own hand, something that I'd put time and effort into creating.

January continued slowly, a dark, dank, depressing month and the first month of a second year without John. The previous January he'd still been here. If only I'd made contact when I bought that stupid phone and my head was so full of panic. If only I had another chance to put everything back together again. If only we were beginning a 'normal' year together.

I remain eternally grateful for everything that I've been shown, and for everything that I have, but sometimes I think that normality would be nice. To turn back the clock and the calendar 20 years, to a time when we were just a normal pair of teenagers. But then, I ask myself, were we ever?

Later that month, Mum returned home one day to find John sitting on the coffee table in the living room waiting for me.

'What are you playing at?' she said. 'You startled me.'

He vanished promptly.

I arrived at about lunchtime. Aware he was now invisible but still in the room with us, she began to explain how she wanted to get the house organized again now that Christmas was well and truly over.

I've had my last Christmas, he butted in, *and it was terrible because I felt so ill.*

Mum was stunned into silence.

'Oh John, why did you have to go and die and leave us feeling so awful?'

I didn't want to die. I thought they were going to get me better. With that remark he disappeared from Mum's until the end of the month.

When he did return he seemed particularly anxious to see me. Robin and the girls had made plans to go out for the evening, so I decided to watch a video with Mum at her house. I often visited during the day but never at night, as I'm always at home with the family.

Mum phoned me earlier in the day to say that John's presence was more pronounced than it had been in a long time. 'Every time I turn around he's there. *It's the twenty-third today*, he said. *Two for me and Amanda, and three for the three of us. I can't wait for tonight. It's been years since the three of us spent an evening together. I just can't wait.* He's so excited he's making me dizzy.'

That news excited me. I began to prepare myself like a teenager going on a first date. I wanted to dress up for him. I felt young and alive again.

I arrived at Mum's brimming over with anxiety and anticipation. My stomach was filled with butterflies, and as soon as I set foot over the doorstep, his loving presence greeted me.

'He's here now,' I said with a sigh of relief. I gazed into the living room and smiled in awareness that he was standing just paces in front of me. The atmosphere once again was charged with love. He drifted towards me and began to stroke my face. Affectionate gestures of this kind persisted throughout the evening, causing me to giggle and smile repeatedly. I removed my wedding ring again at his request. For one night at least I belonged entirely to him. That simple act could erase the last 20 years. In some ways it was just like it used to be. To have him caress my body in that very room with such devotion took me back a long time, except that part of him would now always be missing, and it's that missing part that leaves me with such perpetual sadness.

I lowered my gaze to the floor and remembered the times when I could see his love-filled eyes staring back at me, or feel his head resting gently on my knee. Now I could see nothing, could touch nothing, and I longed more than anything to throw my arms out into space and hug where there was nothing to hug except space.

For mum the climax of the week would come three days later, on the 26th January, 26 years after my grandmother's death. Mum had been preparing some dinner when she heard a 'tap tap' sound from the porch. Someone was knocking on the inner door. She looked up to see a dark, shadowy figure and assumed it was Dad returned from his daily walk. She opened the door to let him in. It wasn't dad but John, and he passed straight through her just like the last time. She turned to the living room and saw him sitting as usual in my chair. My grandmother was on the sofa. Stunned by the apparition of both spectres, she took herself to sit between them. No one spoke. My grandmother, despite being eaten way with stomach cancer at the time of her death, looked remarkably fit and well. Within a couple of minutes both apparitions vanished, leaving Mum with goosepimpled arms and legs like jelly.

It seemed John had brought her to visit, but how? My grandmother died before John and I even met. He knew nothing about her, and yet after 26 years, during which time Mum had never experienced any evidence to suggest any form of after life, John had been able to bring her to my mother's house. Why did he have the power to do what my grandmother couldn't? 'You're going to think I've gone completely mad, now.'

'Why?'

'Well, it's ridiculous, but I was sitting up in bed watching breakfast television, when this white goat with massive horns walked into the room, and just stood there'. We both began to laugh. 'I rubbed my eyes hard, and looked again, but it was still standing there in front of me. It stayed for a few more seconds, then disappeared.'

'Well,' I said, 'a white goat is a symbol of something, isn't it? I'll see what I can find out.'

I returned to the library to look for more clues. A goat with large horns represents masculinity and virility, but it still didn't explain to me why John had appeared as one; and it was him, it had to be.

I needed to make another trip to the cemetery as it had been several weeks since the last visit, and I knew John's family wouldn't have bothered much during the bad weather months. Just before we drove through the gates, Mum and I had been discussing an article I'd read recently, on how deceased loved ones can appear to you within 24 hours of your own death. She interrupted me abruptly.

'Remember exactly where you are as you're telling me this,' she said.

'We're just outside the cemetery, roughly in line with John's grave.'

Later, when we got back, I insisted she explain. 'When you were talking about deceased loved ones putting in an appearance,' she said, 'I turned towards you and caught sight of the white goat in the back of the car. It was sitting right behind you! I know it sounds too ridiculous to be true, but it was most definitely there. I couldn't tell you then, because you'd have turned around and probably caused an accident. I don't know what's happening to me any more. I keep telling him to leave me alone. I'm too old for all this.'

Over the next few weeks all my concentration was focussed on designing a valentine wreath, and how I would be able to get it to the cemetery after Karen had left her tribute. I had some flowers that were slightly past their best, so I took them to John's grave the day before and placed them in the centre. I would return the next day with a proper tribute.

On the morning of the 14th, I arrived at Mum's with some red roses and white gypsophila ready to begin. Once again the cold weather numbed my fingers as I set to work in the back garden. I incorporated some prickly bits around the outer edge of the heart, knowing that whoever picked it up would not find its removal such an easy task. I'd become angry at the thought of my flowers and pots being repeatedly stolen. I left my visit as late as possible, hoping that Karen would have already left her tribute and our paths wouldn't cross. As soon as I arrived, a small bunch of red roses told me that she'd been and gone. My yellow and purple carnations were nowhere to be seen, neither were the crocus bulbs that I'd planted the previous autumn. One or two blades of green were just noticeable as they emerged from that waterlogged earth between the weeds, the tops clearly cut off. What a spiteful thing to do.

I lovingly placed my heart in the centre and prayed it would last the week. I was delighted the following Monday to see it still there. It remained in place for five weeks, during which time I made two further visits, each time leaving bunches of flowers in containers dug well into the ground. With every visit I made, I felt more and more like a criminal. I whizzed in and out as fast as I could, my heart pounding, hoping I wouldn't be seen.

How would a married woman explain her visits to another

man's grave? It would be assumed that John and I had been having an affair, when in reality I'd remained faithful all these years. Since the day I first met Robin. John and I had never even shared so much as a kiss. I shouldn't have had to be sneaking around as I was. Why did I always have to sneak around? Even before I was married I had to sneak around just to be with him. When was it all going to stop? I found myself in a perpetually belligerent mood over feeling so guilty just because I left flowers on his grave. I had more right than anybody to leave flowers; he'd requested it. Why couldn't I shout out my good news to the world at the top of my voice? He is mine! We belong together!' I had no choice but to conceal my emotions, letting them fester like an infected wound.

The next month began with Mum going to Scotland to stay with my sister and my niece Florence for a few days. Dad decided to stay at home. It would soon be a whole year since John's death. On Tuesday, 5th March I was sitting quietly in the living room with my cup of tea and my wistful thoughts when Kimberley blasted in through the door.

'I swear this house is haunted! I've just seen it again in the hall. I'm not crazy, Mum, I really did see it!'

'What, the ghost?'

'Yeah, just like the last times. He walked from the porch into the hall.'

'What did he look like?' I asked. Robin was listening.

'I don't know really, but he was wearing blue.'

Robin stayed silent, but gazed upwards from his newspaper briefly in disgust, as if we were a pair of escaped lunatics.

I knew John had been with me all evening, and now he'd proved it once again in a dramatic way.

My biggest shock was still to come. Mum returned two days later and I was there to welcome her. I sat myself down in preparation for what she was about to tell me. Her eyes were brimming with excitement. 'I've seen him,' she said. 'I've seen him properly. The weather was terrible, torrential rain all day, and so dark. It was Tuesday, Florence was due to arrive home shortly on the school bus, and I was walking along this long, lonely, straight road to the drop-off point. There was no one else in sight, just me. Suddenly I was aware of a man in the distance walking towards me. He was middle-aged, with dark hair and glasses, but I didn't really see where he came from. There wasn't really anywhere he could have come from, because the road was completely straight. One minute there was no one in the road, the next he was just there. As he passed by he spoke to me. "Awful weather!" he said. "Yes. Better now the rain has stopped." I replied. He continued to walk on. "For now, it'll probably be back." As I turned round in anticipation of his reply it was John's face staring back at me, exactly as he was, as he used to look when we all worked together. He spoke with a distinct Scottish accent.'

'Don't you remember, some words he came out with were very Scottish-sounding, and when he was at home with his family his accent became even more pronounced.'

'You're right, I remember now. Well, anyway, it was him. No doubt about it. I hadn't even been thinking about John, and at first it didn't dawn on me who it was. It all happened so quickly, and by the time I realized what I'd just witnessed, and turned back round for a second look, he'd vanished. There was nowhere he could have gone to'.

'You really saw him?' I asked.

'Yes, I really did. But the strangest thing was he appeared so real. I've seen him many times around the house in ghost form, although his face has never been really clear, but this time was different. He was "in the flesh".'

'What was he wearing?'

'A raincoat, a blue raincoat. Yes, navy blue.'

'You're sure it was blue?'

'Yes, quite sure. Why?'

'And this was on Tuesday? Definitely Tuesday?'

'Yes, I told you.'

'Kimberley saw him on Tuesday night in our house wearing blue.'

'That's extraordinary!'

'Isn't it though? And do you remember what you said to me last year, not long after he died?'

'What?'

'That one day, when it was wet and dark, you would see him in his full image, exactly as he was.'

'I did, didn't I? I used those exact words.'

'What about the stranger that you saw first?' I asked. 'Was it a real person? Did you see John through a real live person, or was the stranger a ghost too?'

'Because the person vanished completely, I think John must have somehow appeared as someone else at first, then as himself. The person I saw first wasn't John, but then he turned into John. It's all very weird isn't it? I asked him "why here, now?" *I always do the unexpected*! he replied.'

What I found amazing was the fact that for nearly a year now, John had been communicating to us only by a form of telepathy. This last encounter had proved he was able to speak, or at least appear to speak, as we do. This changed my whole concept of death. We always believe the dead to appear as ghostly apparitions, not living, physical beings like us. How much power do the dead really have? And how big is the divide between the two worlds?

The last time I saw John alive, the voices had told me I would see him again before my own death. I had been imagining that this would be in a 'different form', not the one that I had known. Yet all the voices had said was that I *would* see him. Now I knew that there is only one way to see him, and that is as himself. He's still the same person in every way, he's still John. Death hasn't changed that.

25

March drifted onwards, and I was aware it would soon be Easter. Last year it had been Easter week when we'd attended John's funeral. This year Easter was early. It would fall on the weekend before the anniversary of his death. I knew that being so religious his family would visit the grave on Easter Sunday, and then again for the anniversary three days later. My challenge was to somehow work around their plans.

I would leave some flowers the day before Good Friday, then the day before the anniversary I would take a flower-studded cross.

The week before, I was working on the book when the computer key seemed to lock. Nothing would come up on the screen and I soon realized supernatural influences were taking over. A letter 'd' appeared, followed by dozens more. My hands were raised from the keyboard, yet the letter 'd' continued to materialize on screen. It was out of control, working by itself. I knew John had another message for me, and tried to figure it out. What could the letter 'd' signify? Could it be 'decoy'? Was it date? It was the anniversary of my marriage, the 30th March. *Devastated*, a voice came to me – the day I got married he was feeling devastated. I still couldn't work out why more than one 'd' had appeared.

I made up my mind to put something in the local paper on the 3rd April. Why shouldn't I make my feelings clear? It meant travelling to the next town, giving a false name and address, and paying by cash. It had to be executed with the utmost secrecy. I didn't want to be incriminated in any way, if enquiries were made by Robin, or John's family. I felt more like a criminal than ever.

My next problem, was that it would be impossible to prevent Robin from reading the newspaper. He bought one every night, and always scoured every inch of it. He'd know straight away this tribute was written by me, and indicated a love still going on.

I began to feel quite ill as time drew nearer to 3rd April. The day before, I set to work yet again. The cross didn't take too long. The base I covered in white chrysanthemums, and for the centre, I used a spray of yellow roses, blue irises and white carnations, with a couple of sprigs of ivy. Mum spent the whole morning making a mixed bouquet of flowers. I had also bought a couple of plants and a bunch of red roses.

When we arrived at the cemetery, the first thing we saw was a boy sitting on a bike a couple of rows behind John's grave, staring at us. At first we didn't take too much notice, thinking he must be visiting another burial site, but it became more and more evident over the next fifteen minutes that he was interested only in what we were doing.

'What's he up to, do you think?' Mum asked.

'I don't know. I hope he's not one of those kids who vandalizes graves.'

'Don't look at him,' she said. 'Just ignore him and he'll probably go away soon.'

He didn't, until we'd finished, and everything was in place, when he and his bike disappeared.

The following day began with a visit to hospital. Robin's mother had been admitted two days earlier with heart problems, and had been placed in the intensive care ward. She'd requested a visit, and a change of nightwear, so mum and I obliged, though this meant that both of us were in the hospital yet again, the same one where John had died exactly one year earlier, and on the same ward. This last visit struck me as more unbelievable than any of the others, and there had been so many, all number-related. We had now been to hospital exactly three months following

John's death, four months after, seven months after, and one year after.

In the afternoon, I waited anxiously for the delivery of the newspapers, and the publication of the poem I'd written. It would soon be on view for everyone to see, including Robin. As soon as I could I rushed out to buy one. Both Karen and John's mother had put something in, though neither was a particularly loving message. His brother and sister had too. Mine stood at the bottom of the page, dominating the column. I was pleased. It expressed everything I wanted to say. Now all I had to do was wait.

I left the newspaper at Mums and went home. When Robin did arrive he was without newspaper. I knew this meant he'd seen it. He said nothing and I said nothing. I had no intention of asking for the paper. I had to act completely normally and to the best of my ability I did, though my head thumped and my stomach remained knotted as he stared at me intently during the course of the evening. Much to my relief he said nothing.

The next morning I returned to the cemetery to see what had been left. As I slowed the car, I gasped in astonishment; and my heart sank. Every plant and flower we'd left had gone, including the cross. In their place was a small floral arrangement in a basket, and two bunches of flowers with the wrapping still on, one from John's brother, and one from Karen.

I was boiling over with anger and frustration. I opened the nearest dustbin to see Mum's and my hard work tipped upside down, thrown in with ferocity, not just placed inside. It was heart-breaking to see so many flowers deliberately and viciously smashed and bruised.

What could I do now? The plants were battered and broken, as was my spirit and faith in human nature. I retrieved my cross and tried to mend it, placed it back in the centre of the grave, and moved Karen's to the side. I was fuming.

I drove to Mums. She was even more shocked than I was, but said, 'you shouldn't have put the cross back. I think you should go back and remove it.'

At first I didn't agree, but once I'd had time to calm down, I began to see things more clearly. Whoever was doing this was turning John's resting place into a war zone, and that wasn't right. God teaches us forgiveness. I had to find the strength to rise above these acts. I made the decision to return and remove the cross. It wasn't an easy task. My head was so full of malice, but it was a question of letting the good inside me rise above the bitterness. I placed it reluctantly back inside the dustbin, and put Karen's back in the centre, as it was before. My consolation was that John could see clearly who had commited these acts of depravity, and that it was wrong.

Next, I had some thinking to do: should I continue with my visits, or should I abstain? I had learned from this experience that evil should never be allowed to prevail over good. It was right that my flowers should be on John's grave. John had departed this world, and couldn't put his wishes forward, so I had to carry them out on his behalf. Real love is about desiring someone else's happiness above your own, and being able to bring about that happiness no matter what the cost.

I strive every day to do the right thing. All my life I believed that you don't have to go to church to speak to God, you can tell him how you're feeling wherever you are. He will listen in the most humble of places. Better that you don't go to church but try to live your life in the right way endeavouring to be a better person, than to go religiously every Sunday just to say you've been. Some people think they can be wicked and spiteful during the week, because a visit to church will make everything right. The next week they begin the same chain of events under the impression that it doesn't matter how bad they are because God will forgive them on Sunday. That's not what it's about. We all make mistakes, we all do things we regret. That is how we learn to be better individuals, but unless we feel remorse for what we've done wrong, then we've learned nothing.

Mum and I became convinced that the boy we'd observed at the cemetery had been told to watch John's grave, and report on who had attended and what had been left. How else could anyone have been so certain the flowers were left by us? I would let things settle down a bit before my return.

I now began to realize the significance of all the 'd's on the computer screen. *Don't, dreadful, destruction, devastation, disaster, demolish:* these words were suddenly flooding into my head.

Robin dropped a hint about my newspaper entry. In reply to something my younger daughter had been saying he answered, 'I know many things about many people, and if I don't know I make sure I find out!'

'What are you talking about?' I asked.

'I know, that's all,' he replied.

'Know what?'

'I know something that you don't think I know about, but I do.'

Right, I thought. And you don't know, that I know you know!

By the end of the month, John made more appearances at Mum's. Once again she was disturbed by a tapping sound on the front door, and stepping outside almost fell over him, as he crouched down on the path before fading into nowhere. I remembered with fondness how he frequently knocked on doors and windows, then ducked down so as not be seen.

He once appeared as a black kitten for a few seconds before running under Mum's chair, and he continued with his quirky little pranks at my house also, like the time when the CD compartment closed by itself, and started to play without me touching it, or when I left a pinched foil cake case on my tea plate and it began to rock back and forth as if being blown by a strong wind.

Then there was the night when I'd been watching television for some hours and suddenly wondered what the time was.

It's five to twelve, came the reply.

John had obviously been in on my thoughts once again.

'I, was under the impression there was no concept of time where you are?'

I can still tell the time you know. It's five to twelve.

217

Anxiously I ran down the hall to take a look at the Grandfather clock. It was midnight. John appeared to be wrong, but just then I glanced at the cooker clock in the kitchen. It was exactly five to twelve. I remembered that the hall clock was five minutes fast. My jaw dropped in astonishment and I let out a surprised snigger. The next morning my daughter asked me who West Ham were playing on Saturday.

'Absolutely no idea,' I replied casually as I continued washing dishes. *Chelsea,* said the voice in my head.

'That's right mum, I've remembered, it's Chelsea!'

And then there were the serious times. The times when we just savoured the moment, and each other. Times when we realized just what a remarkable and unique bond we both shared and how precious every second of time spent together was.

During the first half of May, we experienced a savage downpour. A hot sticky afternoon and John had been tickling my face and teasing me with short bursts of cool air. The roar of thunder filled the skies and the room lit up like a beacon. Spears of rain launched from blackened clouds while a howling wind vibrated the timbers and smashed bushes into the window pane. Then I was reminded that this probably wasn't a storm after all, but the souls of two long-lost lovers merging with explosive ecstasy; not merciless rain cascading onto deserted streets, but tears of exquisite joy as they were reunited for all eternity. You could feel their passion, you could taste the love as that electrical current created its radiant flashes across the sky. It was a celebration in heaven, that day.

'Will the skies light up for us one day, John?' I whispered.

One day soon, he replied. My eyes held fast to the space immediately in front of me. He's staring back. The coldness intensifies. My heart is dancing and my spirit exposed, my mouth tingles gently as he moves closer. Tiny impulses rage feverishly through my body and my lips begin to throb to the memory of his kisses. They reach out in vain to a chilled, invisible cloud of vapour, and nothing.

'Oh John! You have no idea how hard it is for me. You've left it all behind. You don't have to suffer any more.'

I suffer every day I see you with him.

'When you enter the room I hear nothing else and I feel nothing else, except your love. It's just you and me. Just us, just this. You give me a little piece of heaven. Why did you have to die? I love you being here with me like this, but I didn't want you to die.'

I had no life without you.

'I know. I'm sorry. While I played happy families you went on a voyage of self-destruction. I'd do anything to take it back.'

The storm faded into the distance.

26

One year later, I discovered that time moves by no quicker. Life goes on they say, but they are wrong. Existence goes on, long after life has ended. The ability to eat, drink, sleep and work continues as before, when enjoyment, happiness and fulfilment have long ceased to be. Let no one ever tell me that time is a great healer. Time will never heal these deep and open wounds of mine.

When my younger daughter's friend came to stay with us overnight. It should have come as no surprise to me when they both suddenly burst into the living room with white faces and voices trembling with excitement.

'Mum, Lauren wants to know if our house is haunted.'

'Why?' I asked suspiciously.

'Because she's just seen a white cat in in my room. Then she went into the bathroom and saw a man in a black suit!'

'That's right,' said Lauren. 'I didn't imagine it.'

'I don't believe you did. Don't let it worry you,' I replied. Probably easier said than done. The poor girl seemed particularly nervous at the thought of having to sleep in what was evidently a haunted house. I suppose it gave them both something to talk about to their friends at school next day.

John had now been seen by Mum, Kimberley, Florence, Lauren and me. Could five of us all be wrong?

He made another appearance at Mum's on the day before I was due to depart for my summer holiday. Mum had become aware of something dark on the hall carpet. As she bent down to pick it up, it shot away from her hand at great speed. She raised her head to see John sitting on the living room sofa, as vividly as the day she'd seen him in Scotland.

'What are you doing? You frightened me.'

I had to come today, he replied, *it's the last time!* and he vanished instantly.

I was worried sick by that reported remark. Did this mean that he wasn't coming back? But no, only that he'd be coming on holiday with me, so it would be the last time he was in Mum's house for a while.

He touched me intimately while we waited to board the aircraft, then again throughout the flight and the entire week away. He'd be with me during breakfast, then disappear for the rest of the day. He always seemed to return around the time of my evening meal, then vanish again before bed, only to wake me in the middle of the night.

This is the pattern he'll follow at home too. When I'm really lucky he'll stay the full 24 hours. Whenever he's not fully with me I begin to feel anxious and uneasy. He returns as soon as he can. Sometimes he might not speak to me for weeks or months even. I talk to him sometimes but he doesn't answer. At other times he might just suddenly reply to something I've said. I never know when this will occur or why. Whether this is because he's changed in some way and he's not able to communicate as he did before, or whether it's because he's not permitted to now, because we've discussed all the important issues that needed discussing, I don't know. As long as he stays with me, I'll be happy.

The most difficult thing to accept is the unknown. Not knowing where he's gone to or when he'll be back. Whether I've upset him in some way by something I've said or done. Not knowing what he's thinking. Having no control. He has the upper hand and sometimes acceptance comes hand in hand with frustration.

One night he'd been stroking me in the usual way in bed, when all of a sudden the sensations ceased. Several minutes went by. He must have gone to sleep, I thought to myself, then what am I saying? He doesn't need sleep. *Yes I do*, he answered.

'Oh John, what kind of world do you go to?' I asked in wonder.

A world that waits for you. he replied affectionately.

'You say the loveliest things. You ALWAYS say the loveliest things.'

In a quiet moment of reflection I made another important numerical connection. John had made three significant appearances to Mum this year. The number of days between the first and the second was 37. The number of days between the second and the third was 77. The difference between the two is 40. This was amazing.

At the end of June I made my usual trip to the cemetery, but this time something took me by surprise. In place of a weed-infested mound of soil, there was now a grey marble surround and elaborate headstone with two brass vases on either side filled with an outstanding array of flowers in every colour. Could it be I'd come to the wrong grave? I was speechless, yet delighted to see that John had at long last got what he deserved.

I continued with my visits, now leaving floral sprays in foam rather than bunches of flowers in pots. Towards the end of July I left one such mixed display. It was the first arrangement that I didn't construct at Mum's. I set to work in my own back garden that day, but all was not well. John hadn't been his usual enthusiastic self, and I sensed something was wrong. It was just as if he didn't want me to take it. Still I was pleased with the result, so I carefully placed it into the boot of the car and set off. For the first time since my visits began the cemetery was buzzing with people, and cars were pouring in and out. A massive funeral; what awful timing! I decided to drive around the block once or twice, as it appeared to be nearing its end. Each time I went past it was still well under way and I couldn't take the risk of driving through the gates and being seen by someone, so I drove all the way home, then back again. I kept thinking it was a bad omen, and I wasn't meant to go that day. Eventually I managed to leave the flowers, but as it turned out, I needn't have bothered.

The next day Mum had an important message for me, which

came to her in the form of a dream. 'You're wasting your time taking flowers up there,' she said. 'They're being removed as soon as you leave them.'

'Don't be silly,' I laughed, 'they couldn't be. No one has any idea what day I make my visits.'

'In last night's dream you were putting flowers on the grave, and that boy, the one that watched us before, was standing near the dustbin with his bike. As soon as you'd gone he removed your flowers and binned them. John was telling me that you're doing it all for nothing. That boy is removing those flowers as soon as you leave them. He must be going there every day after school to see what's been left.'

'I don't believe that. No one would keep that up.'

'I'm telling you, I know this as surely as you knew he died from AIDS. You don't have to prove anything to him any more. He knows how you feel. You should stop this now.'

I'd also had a dream, in recent days, of taking flowers to the grave only to find that the grave had vanished. I relayed this to mum.

'It's all gone' she told me. 'He's telling me that he's not there anymore. That's finished – his body, his life on earth, the relationship with Karen. He isn't there. He's moved on. He's somewhere else. There's no point to it.'

'I left some flowers yesterday.'

'Well, I'm telling you, they are gone!'

I decided to go back and look for myself, so I called in on the way home. My lily spray had gone in less than 24 hours, just as Mum said it would have. *You're too predictable*, John told me, and maybe he was right. My routine had been far too inflexible.

At first I was reluctant to stop taking the flowers. I had planned to leave well alone, for a while, then come back in between our birthdays, but I sensed that Mum was right. He didn't want me to visit the graveside now. I really didn't need to prove my love any more.

Rest in peace? That's a joke, that is! he said to Mum distinctly one day, as he flitted around the house. The last thing I wanted to do was make him unhappy, so for the time being my cemetery visits and floral displays ended there.

My decision was right. John grew closer to me than he had been in weeks.

One of my fondest memories of these last few months was of waking in the early hours one morning with John beside me. All was quiet. I pulled up the duvet and snuggled in tightly. An incandescent moon began to filter through the gap between my curtains, spreading its fountain of light onto my crumpled pillow, radiant and awe-inspiring. The world was so still, my soul enchanted, and my pulse racing. Earthly paradise.

The hall clock struck four times. I was drunk with tiredness, and never happier as John's gaze stirred my wetted eyelashes, and wakened my sleep-filled eyes to daybreak. His weightless arms around my shoulders emanating such warmth. He was smiling but I couldn't see; becoming closer but I couldn't touch, brushing my body with his. Invisible, yet very real and very sensual – very him. For those next few hours before I drifted back to sleep, the world was ours again and I reflected on past tender moments together, so many and so far away.

'Do you recall our walks home in the middle of the night? I never felt more alive than at that hour, and in the most severe of weather conditions. The autumn leaves raining down on us from the trees overhead in a cascade of purples and reds. You'd unbutton my blouse on that midnight walk, and slip your icy fingers inside. Never remembered much after that; I'd been taken out of myself. The owl hooting in the distance as he watched our mating ritual. A truly magical time, wasn't it?'

Deathly silence brings comfort to my spirit.

'And my room, do you remember my room? An Aladdin's cave of Beatle memorabilia, emerald green paper lantern, complete with emerald green light bulb, the air filled with the overpowering scent of jasmine joss sticks and body spray. My book of sexual techniques ready and waiting on the bedside shelf. A pretty sordid environment, yet there was nothing sordid about the things we got up to in those few hours spent in that emerald green world.

A sixteen-year-old girl with the world at her feet, huge round spectacles, Victorian bloomers and open arms; she's here again just for tonight, minus the glasses, the cheap aroma and the emerald hue. But still here, still bowled over by you. Will you lie down beside her like you did 20 years ago and open up her heart?'

I perceive a prickling sensation on the side of my neck and giggle to myself. 'Thought you were giving me a love-bite, just then.'

You're a bit old for that, aren't you? he replies.

I smile inwardly to that characteristic remark. 'This is what it's all about, isn't it? Lying here with you. Bathing in the moonlight. Silent memories.'

Silent memories, silent thoughts. He doesn't have to answer, it's enough that he's here with me, and I can drift back off to sleep draped in that familiar cloak of love.

Since these these strange events began, Mum and I have concluded that we rarely dream of those close to us who have died. When such people do appear in our dreams they never make conversation, prompting us to ask, 'Why do the dead not speak?'

However, exactly seven years after my uncle's death, Mum encountered three dreams on three successive nights. In the first she was conversing with my dead grandmother. The second saw her conversing with my dead uncle and aunt, and the third with a family friend who had departed some years before, and was 'just passing' when he felt he had to make a visit. In my last dream I was conversing with John himself. 'But you're dead!' I told him when he suddenly arrived from nowhere.

'I know I am,' he confirmed, 'but they let me come back!'

We kissed and made love. It was so real I could feel the warmth of his skin when we touched, and the familiarity of tone in his voice when he spoke. The conversation that followed I understood at the time to relate to the world he's in now, and the fact that he'd been permitted to return to this world to be with me. Some 48 hours later, I realized he'd been talking of a previous existence. 'It's pretty boring here you know?' he'd said. 'There's nothing much to do, nothing to read. We did have a queen.'

'Did you?'

'Yes. There was a queen, but she ran away because she was having a baby. She went away so they killed all the people, but I was allowed to come back. Everyone was killed, but they let me come back!'

He was talking about his life before we met. He had been allowed to come back so we could be together. In every dream I'd had about John since his death we had never actually spoken face to face. This was the first time. I woke up to John's distinctive touch. He was right there with me, and I knew immediately he'd tried to tell me something of great significance. Did such a queen exist? I asked myself. Did she have an illicit affair which resulted in pregnancy? Were all the people killed? And if so, why? Most importantly, why was John permitted to return?

Eleven days after the dream, in the eleventh month, and for the first time in many weeks, we had a proper conversation. I had returned to bed for my usual half-our nap after seeing the girls off to school, when John's voice began to seep into my thoughts. *Do you remember how it was?* he said. *We did have a baby, don't you remember? It was a long, long time ago. You ran away.*

'Like in the dream?'

You were the queen. You were having my baby and you went away,

'I did? I was really a queen?'

A great queen.

'Where?'

Egypt.

'Did I hear that correctly? And they killed all the people afterwards, including you? What happened to the baby?'

It died.

226

'That's terrible. Did it die straight away or did it live for a while?'

It died at birth. It was already dead. You gave birth to a dead baby boy.

A strange sense of grief passed over me.

You were heartbroken.

'I guess that's why I've always felt this overwhelming need to have a child with you, to replace what we lost. We loved each other so very much, didn't we?'

Remember how it was?

'I can't. It's too long ago.'

Try to remember!

'I've been trying to find out, but I can't find anything on this.'

You've been looking in all the wrong places.

'I suppose that's why we were never allowed to have children in this life; it was our punishment for what we did, like the dead baby.'

He repeated, *We did have a baby, but the baby was dead, and you were so heartbroken.*

'You were allowed to come back? To live again?'

Yes. So were you.

'My poor baby. I'm so sorry. Can you tell me any more? What happened to me?'

No answer. Another voice entered the conversation. I didn't know whose voice it was, but I got the distinct impression it was male.

You remember going away?

'No.'

You went away because of the baby.

'I don't remember.'

You don't want to remember. You had sex with your brother. You were in love with your brother.

'I wouldn't do that.'

But you did. You were ashamed because of the baby so you went away. The baby was born dead. It was deformed. You killed yourself!

'No I would have remembered.'

You don't want to remember because you were ashamed of what you'd done. You had an incestuous relationship with your brother.

'No.'

Queen Nefertiti ran away in disgrace.

'I wouldn't.'

The child was your brother's. The information was buried.

The following morning I checked the internet for information. It appears that Queen Nefertiti disappeared from court after the death of her daughter. No one knows why her name and her image were suddenly removed from record. Some say she was banished, others believe she just left. Her body has never been found. I felt numb. This information left me stunned. To suddenly discover things like this about yourself that you never knew before can be an overwhelming experience. My head was fuzzy, my stomach knotted. I didn't know what to think or how to feel. That afternoon I told Mum what had happened, including something I hadn't previously mentioned regarding John. 'I always believed he was my responsibility, that it was my job to protect him, like a big sister might feel towards her brother. The day of the funeral, when we sat in church and looked at that photograph on the coffin, I felt I was looking at my twin brother. That's exactly what I felt.' Mum was speechless.

That afternoon I also told Mum that in several previous dreams John had spoken to me using phrases I didn't understand. At the time I thought they were Scottish slang words. He confirmed later they were Gaelic. He'd spoken to me in Gaelic, and smiled when I didn't understand. What I did understand was that this was yet another very important and significant connection. There had been the circle of Celtic stones arranged on his grave, and when Mum had seen him in Scotland it had been right next to one of the oldest Celtic cemeteries.

'Perhaps when you die you somehow go back to your roots' she said. Perhaps she was right.

I showed her the tickets that had arrived that morning for a forthcoming David Gray concert. We were both astounded at the seating number I'd been allocated: number 73 in block number 4!

Perhaps just as amazing and baffling is the bond I seem to share with Jeeves. I bump into him on a regular basis, and always seem to know instinctively when it will happen. I can wake in the morning and say to myself, I'm going to see Jeeves today, and I always do. He's often the very first person that I see, and on more than one occasion in past months, while actually choosing the flowers to take to John's grave. Mum keeps running into him too. We seem to be extraordinarily linked to each other by places and events; but what is it all about?

By the end of the following week I was feeling awful. Confused, wretched and alone. Struggling to come to terms with what John had told me, and all by myself.

'John's not been here for days,' I told Mum. 'Not properly; it's getting me down.'

'He hasn't been here either,' she replied. 'It's strange, isn't it? He walked into the bedroom one night last week. I couldn't get to sleep so I got up to make a hot drink. He followed me into the room, nearly causing me to spill my tea onto the bed.'

You know Amanda betrayed me don't you? Left me to fend for myself and make the best of it, 'he said.'

I was upset by this information. That word betray was the exact word used by the voice I heard just after my marriage to Robin. I was betraying John by being with anyone else. Would he ever truly forgive me for what I'd done?

Next day was Saturday, the temperature barely above freezing as I sat in the chilled outbuilding at the rear of our shop working on this book. My fingers throbbed with cold as I depressed each key in turn, endeavouring to transfer my memories onto paper. Sometimes Mum pays me a visit to break the day. I had the feeling today would be no exception, but needed to crack on, so I hoped she'd leave me in peace. John spent the day with me in the usual manner for the first time in ages, lifting me out of my melancholic mood. Just before closing, Mum phoned to ask what sort of a day

I'd had. 'I was going to come and see you,' she said, 'but this voice said to me, *Don't bother, just leave her alone! She's all right today, she's quite happy.* It was John,' she continued. 'He's been here today for the first time all week.'

'Yeah,' I replied, 'here too. And I was happy to be on my own today, quite amazing really as I'd been feeling so low yesterday.'

On 27th December I was in total ignorance that one of my wishes was about to be granted. Two days after Christmas, John woke me in the early hours of the morning, with the usual nose tickle.

Kiss me! he instructed.

I eased my lips into the velvet darkness at his telepathic request and they reached a wonderful, invisible feathery cloud. It was truly magical; the most erotic sensation I ever experienced. We kissed a total of three times in all.

'You feel lovely,' I whispered, as an oblivious Robin slept soundly beside me.

So do you, John responded, *all soft and warm.*

It was indescribable, being able to touch him in such a way. Words could never begin to explain how divinely perfect it was, and how warm and peaceful it left me feeling, a feeling that would lift me high for days after. I sensed this was purely a 'one-off', something that wouldn't be repeated, at least not for a while anyway.

During the first half of January events began to take a very strange turn, coinciding with the submission of my manuscript to publishers. For the first time in months I had been experiencing strong feelings regarding the grave, that perhaps I should make a spontaneous visit. I arrived at Mum's to find her listening to her Daniel O'Donnell CD. 'There's much activity here today,' she said. 'He'd been asking why we haven't been to the grave to take flowers for such a long time.'

'He knows why we haven't been. I thought he didn't want us to go again?'

'He says he wants you to listen to "Danny Boy".'

'Danny Boy? Why?'

'You've got to listen to the words. I'll put it on for you. He says it's in reverse. Tell Amanda it's in reverse. In the song she's singing to him, but John is saying the words to *you*. Do you understand?'

The haunting melody began to fill the room. I listened intently to each and every word. It was the first time I'd heard the complete song. The lyrics were so sad, and it seemed so personal, my eyes began to fill with tears.

'Oh mum, he wants me to go to the grave. To kneel down and whisper that I love him, listen! Then he shall sleep in peace until I come to him. We must go today,' I said.

'I thought you were going to sort out all those book notes you left here last week?'

'I can't concentrate on that now, or anything else. If he wants me to do this then it must be today. We'll have to buy some flowers first.' With a simple spray of roses I headed for the cemetery, doing exactly as he'd instructed through the song. I found the place where he was lying, trod softly over the hushed winter ground, and knelt down to position the flowers. He was waiting for the words. On a gentle breeze they left my lips. 'I love you.'

Afterwards, I climbed back into the car and turned the ignition key. 'Babylon' echoed back at me. Once again, I was stunned.

'Mum, listen. For goodness sake LISTEN!'

'God it's not possible.' she cried.

'It can't be happening, not again, right here and now at the very moment when we're so close to his grave. If we'd spent a few minutes longer choosing the flowers, or I'd spent longer at the graveside, perhaps had another radio station on, we'd never have heard it.'

The following morning John seemed more contented, though both Mum and myself would have an emotionally charged afternoon ahead of us. I'd been wondering about the book when at exactly 3 o'clock my thoughts were interrupted by that familiar voice. *It's good news, they like it!*

Later that evening when returning home from a local restaurant, we stepped from the car and my daughter seemed to lose her footing, stumbling backwards into the bushes.

'Don't go and fall over,' I shouted.

'It frightened me' she replied, looking pale and drawn.

'What did?' I asked.

'A man of course, what d'you think? He darted straight past me.'

By the end of that week Mum had another message from John. 'He wants you to listen to track number 14 from the same CD, it's called "The Rose"' she said.

This time the words gave me the answers to questions I'd been asking myself for years. Once again John was conveying his feelings. He told me why he'd always held back. He was so scared of being hurt. Most importantly he wanted me to realize that when all seems to be lost, and the struggle seems too hard and too long, I must remember that the seed of our love is sown. Winter may be all around, and the flower may be gone, but it will come again and bloom in heaven. I listened and understood.

After this, John's presence began to wane gradually over a period of weeks, and on Saturday 5th April, at 12.05 pm, as Mum cleaned the outside of the living room window sill, the horrible black dog made a terrifying return. As she jumped up in surprise it slithered across the garden in a zig zag motion before disappearing through the gate. 'It was revolting,' she said, 'like a giant slug. As it moved over my foot it felt all slimy and mushy.'

Why, after almost two years, had it re-appeared today of all days? It was Grand National Day. I had married on Grand National Day. It was also the day we learned of John's death.

Later we decided to make another unscheduled trip to the cemetery to see what flowers had been left for the second anniversary. After I'd been to take a look, I told mum to get out of the car, but strangely she refused. Said she didn't want to. I was surprised. A couple of days later she told me why. 'The black dog was lying motionless across the grave.' She said. 'It's head was hanging to one side and it didn't move. It seemed to be dead. I was so frightened I couldn't bring myself to leave the car.'

'There seems to be some kind of battle between good and evil here,' I said. 'For some reason it's happening through us. All three of us.'

'I know.'

'I still don't understand. There's nowhere left to look for answers.'

'The book of revelation,' she confirmed. As the words left her lips the same thought crossed my mind too. This ghostly apparition had now appeared to Mum a total of three times, and from that day on I sensed there'd been some sort of release. As if the demons that had haunted John since his death had finally been laid to rest. He seemed to have found some kind of peace within himself for the very first time.

Death still remains shrouded in mystery. After sharing an intimate relationship with John since 3rd April 2001, I conclude I am in many ways no wiser than before. He continues to change at regular intervals. Many of the things I experienced in the beginning, such as the cool breezes, don't occur now in the same way. Instead I might just become aware of the faintest change in air temperature, and although he still touches me on a daily basis, he often seems further away. The sensations I feel are distinct, sometimes still very pronounced yet sometimes barely detectable. He has found different ways to establish his presence. Mum says this is because he's earned the right to move on to a higher level. Whereas she used to look downwards when conversing with him, now she looks upwards towards the ceiling.

This new type of existence has caused much depression in me of late. Some days I feel out of control. I long for him to touch me in a certain way, but I can't make it happen. He still assures me he'll never leave. I still feel special and greatly loved, but sometimes not knowing why he's changed or if he'll return to his former self, can get unbelievably frustrating.

I ask myself now, after the events of the last 19 months, does anything really die? I look at the perennial flowers in the garden, how they wither, and shrivel each winter, dead on the surface, yet underneath they continue to grow and flourish, returning in spring with more vibrancy than ever before. So it is with the human soul, the root of our bodies.

As I draw to a close I stand once again with my eyes firmly focussed on the building that remains at the centre of my incredible story. The external refurbishments during the last year have added no more charm and warmth to the crudely designed structure than before. The name, taken from a similar purpose built leisure centre in Las Vegas, though with far less razzle dazzle and glitz, and hardly reflecting a true picture of the place itself, stands out in neon lights.

Were the ghosts of lane three vestiges of lost or disturbed souls from a Roman age? Or ghosts from the future of two teenage lovers sweeping through those parts of the hall where they spent their happiest times in each other's company and each other's arms? The most haunted spots were the ones where we shared our most intimate moments. One thing is certain, one day I will return, we'll return together, hand in hand, to smile again and walk these aisles once more, from the valley of light back to the hall of numbers and the key of destiny.

If I could choose the perfect death I wouldn't go quietly in my sleep. I would choose to die in bed, fully awake and with a vase of heavily scented flowers flanking my bedside; for John to sit beside me and take away my very last breath on this earth with a tender kiss.

When God asks me what I've learned from my life I will tell him this; that no quantity of money or material possessions can replace the feeling of ecstasy gained from lying next to the person you love as you bathe together in shimmering moonlight, watch a sunset or absorb the raindrops when they slide over your cheekbones and trickle through your hair as you embrace beneath a November sky, watch harvest poppies bob and sway in an Indian summer or feel the biting wind cut into your face on the coldest February night. Pleasure and pain simultaneously. Life is sharing the wonders of nature with the person you love. Without that there is no magic, no mystery, no wonder. Happiness wasn't basking in a tropical paradise with a sun-tan and a cocktail. Happiness was walking through the snow and ice at three in the morning feeling tired and shivery, because John was there to put his arm around me and keep me warm. Love didn't come in the form of antiques, expensive holidays or a money-filled wallet; it came in the form of a simple heart necklace and the happiest days of my life. Can anyone who's ever experienced the magic and the mystery of true love say, hand on heart, that there is no God? No after-life and eternal reunion for those who have fought so hard, and suffered so much to acquire the knowledge of truth?

As I walk or drive down these familiar streets each day my heart sinks low. I see a former imprint of John and myself on every street corner. It seems that every place here holds a memory, be it good or bad. I can see us walking hand in hand. His piercing blue eyes as they stopped me dead in my tracks before he kissed me beneath the stars. The places where we were most happy, and the places where we cried most of our tears. I can see me pleading with him, arguing with him, dancing with him, holding him. There is no escape, wherever I go. I need to be here, need to be surrounded by these images every day of my life. Part of us both will always be here, forged in time for ever.

Whatever it is that binds us together, also binds us to this town. And what of Mum's house? John said that we belonged there. Will we continue to haunt that building also? Will we be two restless souls that never find peace? Will we be able to take our place in Babylon – absolute, complete paradise, the gate of God? Or will we have the ability to take the best of both worlds?

What can be learned from all this? We have to change our attitude towards death and dying. We see death as an end, when we should be viewing it as a beginning, a new beginning, a time of rebirth, another developmental stage in our existence. So as a baby develops inside its mother's womb until it's fully matured to be born, so the spirit grows and develops within the body, until such time as God sees fit for its release from the physical being.

This story proves that you don't have to be rich or famous, good-looking or intelligent to know love, you just have to believe in its existence, and in the existence of God, because he is love itself. The more we are able to love and to forgive, the closer we become to him, and the more we begin to understand.

From my own discoveries and experience it seems that our whole existence is based around numbers, dates, and time. And coincidence? There is no coincidence. Everything we do is planned meticulously, there is a reason behind our every action. The main structure of our lives is decided long before we are born. The question is, do we have the ability to change anything?

I have thought hard about issues like AIDS. Most of us are of the opinion that it's largely a self-inflicted illness. There's a definite stigma attached to it. But how many of us actually look beyond the obvious? What terrible self-loathing, loneliness or despair lies behind people's actions? Do we ever ask ourselves what has happened to that person to make them feel so worthless? How desperate can someone be for affection, that they are blinded to the inevitable outcome of those actions? When we hear that someone has died from AIDS how many of us can say that we try to understand how they reached such a low point in their lives?

The divide between the living and the dead isn't that great. The dead have special powers, and can appear in many different forms, from human to animal. They're also able to take temporary possession of living animals or birds, but essentially people don't change. They're still the same as they ever were.

John has retained all the same features that made him special when he existed in physical form. He's still as crude, still swears sometimes, still touches me exactly the way he did before, still likes to play the same tricks. We are all distinctive individuals. God doesn't want to change that. If he chooses that we should

236

reside in his eternal kingdom, it is because we are what we are. The way he made us.

As I concluded earlier in the story, the point of life on earth is to learn about yourself, and the effects of your actions on those around you. To make mistakes and to learn from them, think how can I become a better person?

Don't put off till tomorrow what can be done today. If there's someone you really care about, let them know now. It's no good saying, when it's too late, 'if only'.

I still believe that the past is a special place to be, but John gave me the gift of knowing that love is for ever, and the best is yet to come. The sacrifices that we make in this world will enrich our lives in the next. Through knowledge comes wisdom and understanding, through love comes eternal happiness.

This story has no ending because there is no end. Love is without end, and life only ends when you stop loving.

It was a cold crisp night. The stars shone like a million diamonds as they showered us with hope. We embraced the night and each other. The tip of his finger gently rolled down my nose, and the moon kissed us tenderly with its powerful beam.

'One day it will all come right,' I whisper softly.

'I never want to let you go,' he replies with desperation.

'We just have to be patient. Just have to wait, don't we?'

'I know.'

'One day. One day!'

So now I play a waiting game. I pray for the day when the rain stops falling, when I can stand before God and say that I did what he asked of me. I'd like to be able to say that I did it well.

To all of you I say, never stop loving whatever obstacles you find before you. If ever in doubt always follow your heart.

To Mum, thanks for all your help and support through the most difficult times in my life. For being there when I really needed someone, and for conveying all those endless messages from John to me.

To Robin, I'd like to say that I hope some day you'll understand. You were a good husband and a good father. Under the circumstances you gave me the best life I could have hoped for, and I'm sorry for any pain I caused you. It was never my intention.

To my daughter Kimberley, thank you for allowing me my privacy. To get on with this book in the peace and quiet I craved so often but rarely found.

To David, I'd like to say, you once stood up in church and said that the four most important things in John's life were Love, Friendship, Music and Football, though you were never sure which one came first. It was love, it was always love.

As for John, I'd like to look into his eyes and ask for forgiveness face to face. To hold him close and tell him that this time I'll never let go. That our hopes and dreams for this life may be gone for ever, but the love he continues to give is never in doubt. I let go my heart, I let go my head, feel it now, Babylon.

For this book we both paid the highest price. It is my gift to you, and my tribute to him.

As it was in the beginning is now, and ever shall be, *love* without end!

As each new day begins
And darkness turns to dawn
Your love shines all around me,
Once again reborn.
When hours move surely onward
And sunlight floods the sky,
I feel your touch upon me,
You prove you did not die.
Calming wind may whisper,
With raindrops, fall like tears,
Our memories together
Will push back all the years.
And when the day draws to a close,
Watch me while I sleep,
Forever mine, now the time
No more shall I weep.
For you are with me always,
In all I say and do,
And in all things you reminded me
How much I'm loved by you.

EPILOGUE

Thirteen days following my information on 'Nefertiti', a world announcement confirmed that the mummified remains found in tomb KV 35 in 'The Valley Of The Kings', together with an older woman and a young man, bore striking resemblance to Egypt's lost queen. – It appeared that all *three* had been deliberately mutilated after death.